Athlete Brands

How to Benefit from Your Name, Image & Likeness

Kimberly A. Whitler & Jay P. Hodgkins

UNIVERSITY of VIRGINIA | DARDEN Business Publishing

Darden Business Publishing
Darden School of Business
University of Virginia

Whitler, Kimberly A. and Jay P. Hodgkins, authors.
Athlete Brands: How to Benefit from Your Name, Image & Likeness /
Kimberly A. Whitler and Jay P. Hodgkins.
Includes bibliographical references.
ISBN 978-1-61598-210-3

Contents

Players, Parents, Coaches, and ADs

You've Come to the Right Place

Introduction

from Ted White, Founder/CEO of Fair Ball Foundation and Former Deputy Athletic Director at the University of Virginia

As the saying goes, "with great power comes great responsibility." The rights of student-athletes (SAs) to monetize and profit from their name, image, and likeness (NIL) has ushered in an era of tremendous opportunity for them, but with the upside, there are a number of unknowns and some real concerns. That's why the lessons in this book offer essential learning not just for SAs, but for those who care most about their development: athletic directors, coaches, and parents. All of these groups share a critical need to understand and be intentional about the reputation (i.e., athlete brand) that SAs are building.

For years, from the athletic directors' and coaches' perspectives, there have been myriad concerns, the most common being that SAs derail their academic, athletic, and/or career pursuits by focusing on potential, short-term financial gain and missing the opportunity to position themselves effectively for the long term. NIL, if *not* managed effectively, can divert SAs' time and attention away from their sport and their classes, rapidly becoming a disruption. Showing up late to practices, missing classes, or failing to focus on the work of building a superior reputation can have consequences. Reputation impacts whether coaches choose to advocate for athletes in their future endeavors—or not. Faculty can choose to advocate for SAs on the academic and career side—or not. Something an 18-year-old may not realize is that building a positive and strong reputation within their campus network opens many doors and opportunities over time.

Coaches feel tremendous responsibility for the SAs in their care. They want to ensure that their SAs have opportunities, but they are also responsible for putting together a championship environment. That is never easy, and it takes a lot of focus, energy, and team cohesion. Coaches have to walk the line between being supportive of individual opportunities and building a team with the right culture that can compete at a high level. One of my favorite things about this book is that it helps drive this synchronicity—between the individual SAs, their coaches and teams, and their universities. Coaches and athletic directors will appreciate that the book provides encouragement for SAs to seek opportunities, but to do so in a way that is thoughtful and more reflective of their position on the team and their goals inside sport.

Parents' struggle to convince their children to focus on long-term goals is one they have known for generations. While parents are excited about the new possibilities for their children through NIL, many worry that it will become a significant diversion from more important, longer-term opportunities. The most precious resource SAs have is time, and if they divert too much of it toward social media or promotional activities that harm their performance in competition or the classroom, they could be wasting that resource. Much like parents need to help their children find the right program in the recruiting process, they can help their SAs steer toward branding opportunities that advance them toward their true goals.

For SAs, there is no such thing as opportunity without strings attached. Money is almost always given with an expectation of something in return. Those of us who feel responsible for the SA experience want to make sure SAs are given the agency and tools to think through this on their own. We want this new opportunity to advance learning and growth, but most of all, we don't want SAs to get trapped in a bad situation with unintended consequences.

NIL, however, isn't all worry. We're already seeing some SAs earn life-changing financial reward, and even change the lives of others less fortunate by using their profit to advance a purpose. In my view, though, the real gift of NIL is that it will prompt SAs to begin thinking about and building their brands in ways that helps them achieve their goals. Most people don't understand the importance of reputation and brand building until later in life. But athletes have the opportunity to think through this and figure it out now.

Those of us in athletics departments, coaching staffs, and university employees who have responsibility for the SA experience are limited by a patchwork of rules, regulations, and laws in how we can help SAs secure NIL opportunities. No matter what an SA or their parents have heard, SAs have the autonomy to do this for themselves. They have the decision-making power. With that power comes great responsibility for their reputations and futures. Most of us want SAs to take a deep breath, get good advice, and do some research around how to take advantage of opportunities that build their reputations. When Kim Whitler and I first started talking about how to educate our SAs around NIL, the main objective was to create an opportunity for students to do that research, to engage in deep reflection, and to help students find a way to align monetization with their bigger life and career goals.

Through this book, SAs can independently dig deeper to reflect on what matters to them—who matters to them—and who they want to be. When SAs figure this out, then profiting from their NIL becomes so much easier. And the strength of this book is that it offers an easy-to-follow process that encourages SAs to think about their values and goals first, then the athlete brands they want to create to advance those goals, then ways to monetize their desired brands. In other words, it correctly puts the horse before the cart.

Consider Diana Ordoñez, who competed as a member of the women's soccer team at the University of Virginia. As she has thought about who she wants to be, a very important part is helping young women have a positive body image. She is building her brand by creating events, engaging other female athletes, and speaking to young women, all in a manner that supports her longer-term goals. I imagine that the 50-year-old version of Diana will look back with pride at the choices she made at this point in her life and the positive brand she is building. She is aligned— from her goals to her brand to her actions to her monetization. And because of this alignment, a number of companies have reached out to Diana because their efforts align with her brand.

This book can help any SA walk through a similar alignment process. It puts the SA in the driver's seat and gives them agency and control, instead of sitting back and waiting for some online sports website to offer them a free sweatshirt for a lifetime agreement. And empowering SAs to take positive ownership of their reputations is something I believe athletic directors, coaches, and parents can all support.

CHAPTER 1

Heard the One About the Cart
Before the Horse?

Why It Matters How You
Build and Monetize Your Brand

> **Building a successful brand comes *before* an athlete can actually make money off of their brand. The real challenge is in understanding how to create a valuable brand. Those athletes who become skilled in brand building will be able to leverage this knowledge throughout their lives, whether they pursue a long-term career in sport or not.**
>
> —*Carla Williams,*
> University of Virginia Athletic Director

According to a *FiveThirtyEight*[1] analysis conducted before student-athletes (SAs) were allowed to earn money through their name, image, and likeness (NIL), University of Connecticut women's basketball then–freshman phenom Paige Bueckers could have earned $670,783 per year from endorsement posts shared with her huge social media following. And that's just the value of social media influencer marketing, which is only the tip of the iceberg for the SA presented with the opportunity to benefit from the value of their NIL.

So now that the NIL era is here, how will the business world assess how much it is willing to pay each individual SA? The answer is by evaluating each player's brand as an athlete. This, of course, begs the question: What is a brand?

Many people think it's a logo, like Nike's famous swoosh, or maybe a visual associated with a product or service. In truth, it's much more. And in the case of individuals like SAs, an "athlete brand" is really your reputation as an athlete—on and off the field.

The sport you play, the university you play for, and your accomplishments have a lot to do with your athlete brand and the value of that brand. Consider former Ohio State men's basketball player Mark Titus. As a walk-on, he launched ClubTrillion.blogspot.com to blog about his experiences watching games from the end of the team's bench. The site garnered more than 50,000 page views a day, which led to endorsement offers while he was still a student and that he later parlayed into a lucrative media career with ESPN, The Ringer, and more. [2]

Turning such athletic-related endeavors into real income is nothing short of heady. But with the opportunity comes trepidation and risk. As an SA, how can you develop a strong and desirable athlete brand? How can you avoid inadvertently damaging your brand through missteps? And importantly, who can help you understand how to design, activate, and manage your brand in a way that helps you earn income from your name, image, and likeness while achieving your academic, athletic, and personal goals?

The purpose of this book is to help you gain knowledge and skill that enable you to develop and manage your own athlete brand so you have more control over your own destiny. This is in contrast to a model where others—typically agents and marketing agencies—tell SAs what to do.

This book is specifically focused on college athletes and what you hope your athletic endeavors can help you achieve. In reality, each college athlete has goals that are entirely separate from their lives as athletes. The focus here is on the goals and aspirations SAs can pursue through sport, and how those goals should impact how you choose to build, deliver, and monetize your brand. This book provides the lessons you'll need to

leverage your athlete brand no matter what path you choose—whether you want to play professionally, become an Olympian, become a coach, or work in a completely unrelated field.

WHY A BOOK ON BRANDING FOR SAs?

In April 2020, the National Collegiate Athletic Association (NCAA) Board of Governors decided to support rule changes to allow SAs the right to benefit monetarily from the value of their name, image, and likeness. With these increased opportunities, the need to help SAs manage this new landscape is real—this book is a step toward meeting that need.

Soon after the NCAA rule change, Ted White, then-deputy director of the University of Virginia (UVA) athletics department, was approached by companies, individuals, and agencies trying to cash in on the moment by offering to help UVA SAs. He asked important questions.

- "Are our SAs better off trusting their brands to agencies and external marketing organizations?"

- "What is the best way to help SAs build their brands to create maximum value?"

- "How can we protect our SAs from unethical and opportunistic people?"

His next question was perhaps the most telling. He wondered if it would be possible to educate SAs so that they could learn how to think about strategic brand building, enabling them to control their own destiny:

- "Would it be possible for us to develop curriculum that would help our SAs lead agencies, agents, and others in developing the brand they want rather than being told by agencies what to do?"

The answer is: absolutely! You can "play offense" by designing, activating, and leveraging your own brand in a way that aligns with who you are and your aspirations.

For example, White noted many former UVA SAs have leveraged the strength of their brands not only to earn better professional playing opportunities but also to make a significant impact outside of playing their sport. For example, Indiana Pacers star Malcolm Brogdon won the 2020 J. Walter Kennedy Citizenship Award for his commitment to education, gender, and health equality, as well as his support for criminal justice and voting reform. He also established the Brogdon Family Foundation, which supports Hoops4Humanity, an organization that seeks to create access to clean water and education for children and families in Africa, and the JHA Education Project, which focuses on

literacy, mentoring, and infrastructure programs for students in underserved communities in the United States.[4]

Just as importantly, SAs can "play defense." You can learn to protect yourself from unscrupulous people who might want to take advantage of you.

New Orleans Pelicans phenom Zion Williamson spent nearly two years in an extended court battle with a marketing agency he signed with as a freshman at Duke University.[5] The agency sued Williamson for $100 million in damages, arguing breach of contract because Williamson decided to terminate his agreement with the firm when he left Duke to head to the National Basketball Association (NBA). Unfortunately, it was a contract Williamson should never have signed and likely wouldn't have if he had been better equipped to manage his brand.

This book focuses on teaching offense and defense by breaking down the process of designing, building, and monetizing your brand into simple steps that can help you independently design your own brand plan. It is organized into short chapters—"hurdles" that you advance through. Most chapters have an activity to complete at the end before moving to the next stage. The activities are short; however, they will require introspection and thought. While you might be able to complete some exercises faster than their suggested times, if you're breezing through every exercise too quickly, you will miss an opportunity to develop a stronger brand. This book is about investing in you, so don't shortchange yourself!

TRUST IN YOU!

There are two ways to build a brand. One way is to hire a firm that will design your brand and tell you what to do, where to go, what to say, and may even post on social media for you. This can be enticing because you don't have to invest much time or effort. The challenge is that nobody will ever care more about your brand than you will. Even company executives want to "own" the design and activation of their brands. They don't want to leave it up to others. The worry with outsourcing branding is that the brand design won't be "right"—it won't fit who they are or want to be. Executives also want the knowledge that goes with learning how to design their own brand, knowing that it can be useful for their careers.

And this represents the second way: you learn how to design, activate, and monetize your own brand. You become proficient enough to lead others to help you develop your brand. You have enough knowledge to engage in meaningful conversations with agents and external agencies. And you learn to ask questions to ensure you aren't being taken advantage of.

The goal here is to empower you to learn how to build and manage your own brand. This will be beneficial not only in the short term: these tools will continue to help over the decades as your brand morphs, changes, and adapts to new life stages and goals.

It's important to trust the process laid out in this book. Championships are built on a great process. Start at the beginning and go through all the steps. Each chapter and exercise in this book is intentionally designed to build on the previous one. When you're tempted to skip the exercise about allocating your time because

Figure 1. The branding process.

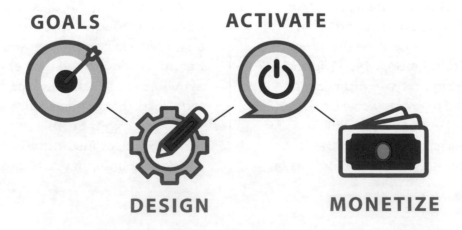

you don't have time…don't! Skipping that step would impact your ability later in the book to allocate time to monetization (meaning making money off your brand).

Figure 1 explains how the book will proceed. There are four primary sections: 1) identify your vision, goals, and resources, 2) design your brand, 3) activate your brand, and 4) monetize your brand.

IDENTIFY YOUR VISION, GOALS, AND RESOURCES

Notice that this process doesn't begin by designing your brand. This is important. Brand design comes after you identify your goals and aspirations, because you want your brand to be anchored on the vision you have for your life. Your brand is a reflection of who you are, who you want to be, and where you want to go, so you must first think about the role of sport in your life and your resources to pursue your goals.

DESIGN YOUR BRAND

Once you understand your vision, then reading Chapters 6–8 will help walk you through a process to create your brand. Based on your vision and goals, you'll understand your

"target audience." Is it your coach, fans, professional coaches, peers, scouts, future employers, sponsors, or somebody else? What do you want to stand for? What value do you hope to create for your target?

ACTIVATE YOUR BRAND

The bridge from a desired brand to a realized brand is your activation plan. Chapters 9–10 will help you understand how to activate your brand to achieve your desired brand image. What will you do to align your actions with your brand?

MONETIZE YOUR BRAND

After building your activation plan, it is time to think about monetization. Notice something important. Most of the book is focused on brand development and activation rather than monetization. As Thomas Rogers, former UVA men's basketball player, said during an interview, "By not focusing on monetization, you put yourself in the best position to maximize monetization."

This is a mistake that some agents make. They start talking to SAs on day one about how they can make money off their brand. This is backward.

It's as if you walked into Lululemon's headquarters and insisted it start selling golf shirts. You can't identify the best money-making opportunity until you understand what the company's business objectives and vision are, what resources it has, what its brand stands for, what its competitive assets are, and whom Lululemon is targeting.

This is a common way that marketers get into trouble, and you don't want to make the same mistake with your brand. Your brand isn't what people think or believe about a pair of shoes or a tube of toothpaste. It's what they think and believe about YOU! Don't jump into tactics before getting your strategy set.

GETTING STARTED

Your time is limited, so this book is designed to be simple and straightforward. Most chapters include exercises at the end for you to complete, as well as sample exercise responses from three different UVA athletes to serve as examples. These athlete role models are

TY JEROME, an NCAA national championship–winning basketball player who now plays in the NBA,

REBECCA JARRETT, an All-ACC collegiate women's soccer player who may pursue soccer after college or become an entrepreneur, and

GRANT KERSEY, a former UVA men's basketball team manager who earned a spot on the team as a walk-on and is now working in sports-related business endeavors.

These examples show that—whether you are an NBA player, a collegiate star who aspires to a different career after graduation, or a team manager who goes on to a career in business—you can apply these principles and exercises to help you achieve your goals!

This process is a beginning step for SAs but an important one. It starts with your goals and vision, moves to your brand strategy, then considers your brand activation and monetization. Your brand is worth the effort!

EXERCISE ONE
Write Down Your "Why"

Before moving forward, take one minute to write down two things: 1) your reason(s) for wanting to invest time in reading this book and completing the exercises (your "why"), and 2) what you hope to get out of the process. This will serve as a reminder of why you started this process and how it can help you accomplish your short- and long-term goals.

WHY YOU ARE READING THE BOOK

WHAT YOU HOPE TO GET FROM COMPLETING
THE EXERCISES IN THE BOOK

CHAPTER 2

Are You All Brains or Got Much Game?

What You Want the Role of Sports to Be in Your Life

> " Any way you can be great at
> doing what you love to do,
> you've got to commit to it.
> You can't want something but
> not put in the work. "

—LeBron James,

four-time NBA MVP, four-time NBA Finals MVP,
four-time NBA champion, actor, and entrepreneur

By the time LeBron James graced the cover of *Sports Illustrated* as a high school junior under the headline "The Chosen One," the only real question about his future was which NBA franchise would be lucky enough to land the no. 1 pick in the 2003 NBA draft.

As an 18-year-old, he famously turned down a $10 million check from then–Reebok CEO Paul Fireman requiring that he sign a $100 million sponsorship deal right away and not talk to Nike or Adidas first. His instinct paid off: he signed a $90 million sponsorship deal with Nike soon after because he believed in Nike's vision for his brand and the value it would create later in his career.[6] In 2015, James re-upped with Nike for a lifetime deal reportedly valued at more than $1 billion.[7]

Then there's UVA walk-on point guard Chase Coleman, who, despite his brother Matt's aspirations to play in the NBA after a stellar career as point guard for the Texas Longhorns, saw a much different path for his future in sports.

"Ever since maybe high school, when I realized playing may not go the way that I really want it to— but I knew my mind could take me to the places I wanted to be— that's when I took more interest to [coaching]," Coleman said.[8]

There are many paths for a college athlete to follow, and the options don't all end in "I'm going to go pro" or "I'm done with sports after college."

Maybe you're like Chase Coleman, and you're envisioning a decades-long career coaching after your college playing career is over. Maybe you want to take a full-time job after college, but you plan to continue training for the Olympics or running camps for young athletes. Even if you aspire to be a professional athlete or Olympian, you probably have some sense as to whether you're considered a sure thing or have some ground to cover. That self-awareness will be critical as you work through the exercises in this book.

Instead, perhaps you plan to hang up your cleats for good when your college career is over. If so, why bother worrying about your athlete brand at all? Well, you'd probably like to perform at a level that will enable you to keep or increase your scholarship for four years, even five, to pay for your education. And your athletic career can also add value to your future non-athletic pursuits. Your athletic brand can be a powerful networking tool in your personal and professional life. More importantly, you can use the brand that you create on the field to accomplish other goals off the field.

Consider Johnny Mishu, a recent graduate of UVA's Darden School of Business. Johnny had played baseball at Princeton and had worked for Major League Baseball (MLB) and the Texas Rangers organizations prior to attending Darden. He also knew that he wanted to pursue a career in business. He decided to interview for brand management jobs while at Darden (essentially, training to be a CEO). His issue? He needed to figure out how to "position" his athletic career and baseball work experience. His answer? He had a winning competitive spirit and he found a way to work with others to achieve unparalleled outcomes. He did this on and off the field. Because he was focused on understanding and designing his brand first, he was able to convert something that might seem irrelevant to businesspeople—his baseball experience—into something meaningful to prospective employers.

The most important thing you must do first is simply this: know yourself. Ask yourself: **What do I want the role of sports to be in my life while in college and after college?** Where am I headed? The journey to develop and manage your brand begins with understanding the answer to these questions.

Consider two examples:

This book's author, Kim Whitler, was a collegiate golfer. She knew that she would be unlikely to be able to support herself after college on golf alone. Consequently, playing golf was her ticket to a free education. While it was significant, her education was far more important, and so she was unwilling to sacrifice either the classes she took or grades for her sport. Her priority was to get a business and psychology degree, with top grades, while playing competitive golf.

Contrast Kim to someone like Ty Jerome, who played on the 2019 national championship–winning UVA men's basketball team. He came to UVA dreaming of playing in the NBA. His priority was to become the absolute best basketball player he could be and lead the team to a national championship. While he was an excellent student and school mattered to him, his basketball aspirations were the priority. Decisions related to what degree to pursue or what classes to take would need to align with his basketball goals.

These two examples describe nearly polar opposite views of the role that sport can play in a college student's life. In the first example, sport is a means to an end (a great business career). In the second, school is a means to an end (a professional basketball career). These decisions will lead to very different

decisions regarding your allocation of resources, brand design and activation, and monetization goals.

EXERCISE TWO
Define the Role That Sport Will Play in Your Life

Using the table, describe the type of role that you want sport to play while in college and after college. Things to consider:

• How important is sport to you during college? Is it the no. 1 priority? Or is it a secondary priority that enables you to achieve other goals? Is your sport critical to be able to afford college (i.e., a scholarship)? Or is it a passion that you love but unnecessary from a financial perspective?

• How important is sport to you after college? Will sport become your full-time job after college, or will it become a hobby that you play for fun?

Once you have contemplated the questions, please write your answers in the blank spaces. If you're curious about how other SAs have completed the exercise, take a look at Rebecca Jarrett's responses following the table.

Role of Your Sport in Your Life

IN COLLEGE

AFTER COLLEGE

Role of Your Sport in Your Life

IN COLLEGE

- My sport is extremely important to me during college. Not only is it my biggest time commitment, but it is also my no.1 priority because I want to become the best player I can be in my time here. I also want to help lead the team to its first-ever national championship.

- However, I am also very intentional about engaging in things outside of athletics wherever I can (including internships, research assistant positions, and entrepreneurial personal projects). Therefore, though it is a priority, soccer is not my only focus at UVA.

AFTER COLLEGE

- Although I can't play forever, soccer has always been (and likely will always be) a massive part of my life. Once I finish playing, I plan to pursue a career in business (specific field and career path to be determined) and I hope to apply many of the skills I developed and leverage the network I have built through my soccer career in my business career. Therefore, I think my sport will continue to enable me to achieve my goals even after I finish playing.

CHAPTER 3

The Importance of
Stretching

Setting (Stretch) Goals You Hope
to Accomplish through Your Sport

> " **Set your goals high and don't stop till you get there.** "
>
> —*Bo Jackson,*
>
> Heisman Trophy winner, former NFL running back, former MLB player, and author

You have identified the role you want sport to play in your life. Did you discover anything new about yourself and your goals? Retired Tennessee Titans linebacker and successful entrepreneur Derrick Morgan said he was in high school when he realized he shouldn't play football just because he was good at it, but because he could win a scholarship to earn a college degree as a "way out" of an environment he felt was too limiting. Even though he was good enough to make it to the National Football League (NFL), Morgan's goals remained centered on using football as a trampoline to improve his family's circumstances.[9] You might be surprised by how many athletes wait until late in their careers before trying the sort of introspective goal-setting that drove Morgan.

In this chapter, you will move from the conceptual to the concrete by establishing what you want to accomplish in your sport and through your sport.

If you examine the brand of Alex Morgan, star of the US Women's National Soccer Team (USWNT) and Orlando Pride, you'll see that the on- and off-field goals she has for her athlete brand are clearly defined. She embraces the expectation that the USWNT will win World Cups and Olympic gold. She leverages the team's success to amplify her own voice in a highly visible and sometimes contentious battle with the US Soccer Federation to help ensure that USWNT pay is equal to that of the Men's National Team.[10]

Off the field, her goal to bring a focus on fun and joy, rather than competition, back to youth sports informs her endorsement, advertising, and social media decisions. As the proud owner of two rescue dogs, she is also a celebrity sponsor of the brand Stella & Chewy's to advance her goal to increase awareness about the need for pet adoption.

BE CLEAR ABOUT WHAT YOU WANT TO ACCOMPLISH

Being clear about what you want to accomplish is important for brand building. Why do you think that is? How might your goals impact your brand-building activities and, importantly, how you might want to monetize your brand?

Consider the following two SAs.

SA 1: A swimmer with dreams of competing in the Olympics. What will he have to do to accomplish his goal? What type of brand might he want to build (and who might he want to influence) that will enable him to more easily accomplish this goal? What is the role of brand monetization in helping him accomplish the goal?

SA 2: A soccer player who wants to be an impact player in college, then pursue an engineering career while continuing to play as a hobby. How might this goal impact the type of brand she wants to build? How important will her long-term athlete brand be (relative to the short term)?

These two different scenarios highlight an important truth: how sport fits in your life and what you hope to accomplish should influence the athlete brand you want to create—and then the monetization choices you make (but that comes later!). For now, it is simply important to understand that how you want to build your athlete brand depends on where you are headed.

There are any number of possible paths that sports can play in your life. The only "right" path is the one that works for you

EXERCISE THREE
Describe the Goals You Hope to Achieve in Your Sport (and through your Sport)

Expanding on **Exercise 2** in the previous chapter, use the table in this exercise to specify the goals that you hope to achieve regarding your sport. Consider the following:

- What are the concrete accomplishments you hope to achieve, in college and after? Ensure that they are specific, measurable, stretch (but still possible) goals. Create general dates to complete these accomplishments. For example, a freshman lacrosse player who hopes to lead his team to a national championship might write, "Win national championship within four years" in the "In College" row. If the player hopes to become a teacher and coach at a high school, he might write, "Become assistant high school lacrosse coach in 5 years and head coach within 10 years" in the "After College" row. How you plan to use your sport can vary significantly. The objective is to think about how it can help you achieve your longer-term aspirations.

It's important to know the difference between ambitious and realistic goal setting. The odds of any high schooler playing in the NFL or competing in the Olympics are quite low. While it is important to be realistic, the few SAs who do end up at the pinnacles of their sports have to have ambition and believe this kind of success is possible. Consequently, you need to decide for yourself what you believe is possible and what you hope to accomplish. It is also reasonable to have a backup plan should the aspiration not end up being achievable.

It's helpful to consider the role of sports in your life as you set goals, so start by briefly rewriting a short paragraph about what you want the role of sports to be in your life in college and after college. Then, create a list of goals you want to achieve in—and through—your sport in college and after.

Goals You Hope to Achieve in Your Sport

**IN
COLLEGE**

**AFTER
COLLEGE**

Role of Your Sport
in Your Life

Goals You Hope to Achieve
in Your Sport

IN COLLEGE

- Create lifetime connection.
- Enhance college experience.
- Vehicle for time management.
- Give back to community.

- National Championship (2018 or 2019).
- Embrace Coach Bennett's Five Pillars.
- Embrace team culture.
- Gain experience in other avenues within sports.

AFTER COLLEGE

- Leverage experience with job opportunities.
- Entertainment value.
- Lifetime personal and professional connections.

- Maintain UVA relationships.
- Work in sports industry after college (2021).
- Gain coaching experience (ASAP after 2011).

CHAPTER 4

You're Not an Unlimited Resource

Allocating Your Time, Effort, and Assets

> " Working hard for something we don't care about is called stress. Working hard for something we love is called passion. "
>
> —*Simon Sinek,*
> best-selling author and inspirational speaker

Until now, you have focused on where you want to go with your sport and what you hope to achieve in and through it. Now, it's time to shift your focus and consider what it will take for you to get there.

Accomplishing your goals requires allocating your resources—time, money, effort, knowledge, network, and so on—in a way that will enable you to succeed. Different backgrounds and circumstances mean that not every SA has the same resources. Just as successful entrepreneurs build businesses based on the resources they have at hand and then adjust goals as their resources change, SAs must do so as well.

Professional golfer Bryson DeChambeau was a physics major at Southern Methodist University who earned the nickname "Mad Scientist" because of how he applied his physics knowledge to his game. He drew international attention in 2020 when he emerged from the Professional Golfers' Association's (PGA) three-month coronavirus pandemic–forced hiatus more than 20 pounds of pure muscle heavier. Amid a torrent of curiosity about his new physique (his shirt size grew from a medium to extra-large), he explained that his study of the game led him to believe that his key to success was creating the shortest possible second shot to the green.[11]

So DeChambeau reallocated his resources—time and effort—during the pandemic to chase his goal: becoming the No. 1 golfer in the world. His formula was a new diet and intense weightlifting to gain size, strength, and swing speed. The result? Longer drives, shorter approach shots, better scores, and more wins.

For his efforts, he was widely mocked. But he got the last laugh when he won one of the first PGA Tour events after the COVID-19 hiatus and then, two months later, won the US Open, his first major tournament victory, by six shots.

HOW YOU CHOOSE TO EMPLOY YOUR RESOURCES WILL DETERMINE WHETHER YOU ACHIEVE YOUR GOALS

Like DeChambeau, how you choose to leverage your resources will impact whether you achieve your goals.

Consider one SA competing in softball who aspires to make it to the Olympics. She spends almost all her free time focused on achieving this goal. She reads about the sport, works out, and prepares herself mentally. She seeks coaching and works to develop those areas where she is weak.

What if the same SA chose to spend a significant amount of her free time trying to monetize her brand? She believes she can make over $50,000 a year as a highly visible athlete investing her free time engaging with fans on social media. She has the same goals and aspirations and is the same person in both scenarios. The only difference is how she allocates her most precious resource: time.

How do you think these two scenarios will play out? Which one makes it more likely the player will achieve her dream of playing in the Olympics?

As a further example, let's examine how former UVA point guard Ty Jerome shifted his priorities between his sophomore and junior years to better align his resource allocation in pursuit of his goals, which included winning a national championship and playing in the NBA after college.

Jerome's Virginia Cavaliers made history as the first no. 1 seed in the NCAA men's basketball tournament to lose to a no. 16 seed when University of Maryland, Baltimore County won the first-round matchup in March 2018. Referred to as "the greatest upset in NCAA tournament history," [12] the loss was devastating for Jerome and his teammates, who had been a dominant force all year, having won both the Atlantic Coast Conference (ACC) regular season championship and the ACC tournament.

After the loss, Jerome's aspirations and goals did not change. He simply changed the way in which he allocated his time. He focused on getting better—better at each practice, better in each game—and shifted how he spent his time during the summer, all of which paid off. "Jerome's persistent shooting practice during the summer—it was rumored that UVA coaches had to kick him out of the gym on some days, to force him to take a break—showed as he scored from around the floor, while his complete court vision allowed him to rack up 202 season assists."[13]

Setting a vision for the future is simply a dream. To make that dream a reality requires aligning your resources with the desired outcome. Anybody can aspire to be an Olympian, but it takes tremendous talent and a desire to invest the time, money, sweat, and tears to achieve the goal.

Among all resources, there is only one we can guarantee everyone has an equal amount of. It's also the most important resource we have: time. Start there, with your time, as you make a plan to allocate your resources.

Identify How You Want to Allocate Your Most Precious Resource—Your Time

One of the not-so-well-kept secrets about time management is that individuals' aspirations for how they *plan* to spend their time differ from the reality of how they actually spend their time. So start with how you actually spend your time. Imagine a typical week during the academic year and fill in every hour of the weekly time allocation chart in **Table 1**. This will give you a sense of how you're currently dedicating the 168 hours that make up your typical week to your main types of activities: athletic, academic, personal/social, and sleep.

Use a word or two to describe each activity: practice, game, class, studying, dinner, sleep, and so on. After the description, add more general categories: **ATH** for athletic activities, **AC** for academic, **P** for personal/social, or **S** for sleep. When you're done, add up the hours for each of the four categories. You may work one or more part-time jobs in addition to your other responsibilities. While work hardly feels like personal time, for the purposes of this exercise, label anything that's not related to athletics, academics, or rest/sleep with a **P**.

Table 1. Weekly time allocation chart.

TIME	MONDAY	TUESDAY	WEDNESDAY	THURSDAY
7AM				
8AM				
9AM				
10AM				
11AM				
12PM				
1PM				
2PM				
3PM				
4PM				
5PM				
6PM				
7PM				
8PM				
9PM				
10PM				
11PM				
12AM				
1AM				
2AM				
3AM				
4AM				
5AM				
6AM				

TIME	FRIDAY	SATURDAY	SUNDAY
7AM			
8AM			
9AM			
10AM			
11AM			
12PM			
1PM			
2PM			
3PM			
4PM			
5PM			
6PM			
7PM			
8PM			
9PM			
10PM			
11PM			
12AM			
1AM			
2AM			
3AM			
4AM			
5AM			
6AM			

Now with that dose of reality, you are ready to plan your desired time allocation. Using the table in **Exercise 4**, decide how you want to allocate your time to achieve the goals you wrote down in the last chapter. Consider the following:

- Start with sleep. There are 168 hours in a week. How many hours of sleep do you need to ensure you are able to thrive? For some people, it might be 9 hours a night— or 63 hours a week. While you don't need to be a sleep expert, every SA should have some understanding of sleep science and the ways optimal sleep links to optimal performance.

- Once you've subtracted available hours for sleep, identify how you want to allocate your remaining time. As an example, sleeping for 63 hours per week leaves 105 hours for academic, athletic, and personal/social endeavors. An SA who aspires to become an Olympian will invest more time in their sport than someone whose primary goal is to use their athletic scholarship to earn a business degree and prepare for a career in marketing. Someone like Grant Kersey, the former UVA men's basketball team manager who wants to work in sports but does not aspire to play professionally, would invest more time in the academic area, but also the social/personal area to build his network.

List your priority activities in each category. This can help you compare priorities across the different categories.

EXERCISE FOUR
Time Allocation to Achieve Goals

To fill out the table, be as specific as possible. For example, you might write "8 hours nightly" as a sleep/rest priority activity, or perhaps you prefer a more complex sleep schedule with 6 hours on weekday nights, followed by 30-minute naps in the morning and afternoon, then 9 hours of sleep on weekend nights. Personal/social priority activities will include the time you allocate to meals, hanging out with friends, playing video games, shopping, and so on. Remember, for the purposes of this exercise, include hours for a part-time job or internship as personal time.

Contemplate your desired time allocation and fill out **Exercise 4**. How do you want to allocate your most precious resource—time—to ensure you accomplish your goals?

SLEEP

Priority Activities

Hours

ACADEMIC

Priority Activities

Hours

ATHLETIC

Priority Activities

Hours

PERSONAL

Priority Activities

Hours

CHAPTER 5

The Good, the Bad, and the Confusing

Identifying Ways Brand Building Can Help You Achieve Your Goals

> " '**Branding' is all the rage lately, but really what it comes down to is this: WHO ARE YOU?** "
>
> —*Lauryn Williams,*
>
> *the first American woman to win a gold medal in the summer and winter Olympic Games and author of The Oval Office: A Four-Time Olympian's Guide to Professional Track & Field*

Congratulations! Your hard work so far has paid off and you've completed the first step in the process: identifying your vision, goals, and resources. By now, you understand the role you want sports to play in your life, your vision for yourself, and the goals you seek to accomplish in—and through—your sport to reach that vision. Those are the fundamental building blocks every product, service, and person in the world needs to establish before becoming successful.

But before you dive into defining, activating, and monetizing your brand, take a moment to expand your field of vision by exploring several examples of athlete brands and ways brand building can help (or hurt) in the pursuit of your goals and vision for your future.

To start, think about what a "brand" is. If you think about Walmart or Amazon, what comes to mind? If you think about Serena Williams, Michael Phelps, or Tiger Woods, what associations—good and bad—come to mind? A brand is the summation of the individual associations that people think and feel when they see a logo or brand name.[14]

The brand of a person—such as a celebrity or athlete—includes what fans, coaches, and others think and feel about the person (whether fair or unfair, reasonable or unreasonable). When everyone's feelings and thoughts about an athlete are aggregated, a singular view of the athlete brand emerges. For example, individual fans have beliefs about Serena Williams. When these individual views are aggregated across all fans, Serena's brand—the defining image held among the target audience—comes into view. This is what marketers try to impact. Over time, they want the target audience's views of a brand to mirror the "brand strategy"—the brand marketers have designed on paper and hope to achieve in reality.

WHAT DO REAL ATHLETE BRANDS LOOK LIKE? THE STRONG AND THE WEAK

Being intentional and strategic about your brand has great potential to add value to your life. That is the promise of a good brand. However, like most things in life, nothing comes easy. Poor behavior in the public eye or failure to maintain brand discipline can create a less-valuable brand. Athletes who skip out on the type of learning contained in this book might create a "confused brand" that lacks clarity and isn't helping them advance their goals to realize their vision.

Take a look at two well-known professional athletes who have what could be defined as stronger and weaker brands. Rather than telling you which is which, read the quotes

from and about these athletes pulled from media and social media activity and try to figure it out yourself. After all, an athlete brand is defined by the impressions others have of you.

As you read, think about these questions: Which brand is strong and compelling? Which feels inconsistent or brings up negative associations for you? For these questions, think about why. For extra credit, take a moment to check out these athletes' Twitter or Instagram accounts. What impressions do you get?

Lydia Ko

In 2015, 17-year-old Ladies Professional Golf Association (LPGA) golfer Lydia Ko became the youngest person to earn the no. 1 world ranking in professional golf. Even long before that moment, she was making headlines that were perhaps paralleled only by a young Tiger Woods. In fact, Ko was so good as an amateur that the LPGA waived its rule that a player had to be 18 before turning pro. Here is a selection of quotes to give you a sense of her brand:

"She made it look easy. She's always had a bit of an individual swing. But she was able to repeat it under pressure. And from 150 yards in, she was deadly."
— pro golfer Annika Sörenstam[15]

"Believe in yourself, believe in your process and everything else will fall in place."
— Lydia Ko[16]

"It wasn't the way I had wanted to finish, but that tournament actually gave me a lot of confidence to say, 'Hey, you know, I can be back in contention.' The more times you put yourself in contention, as time goes by, you're going to be the one holding the trophy in the end."
— Lydia Ko[17]

"She is an outstanding ambassador for our school and a role model to her peers and young aspiring sportswomen and sportsmen throughout the world."
— Lydia Ko's former school principal[18]

Novak Djokovic

Whether you're on Team Rafa, Team Fed, or Team Djoker in the argument over the best player in the history of men's tennis, Novak Djokovic, with his 20 Grand Slam titles (at the time of publishing), is a mandatory part of the conversation. He's also unique in that the three men in the greatest-of-all-time (GOAT) conversation for men's tennis are essentially contemporaries. Rafael Nadal and Roger Federer, who also hold 20 major titles each, are only a few years older than Djokovic and they have all clashed many times—not only in

epic matches on the court but for the attention of fans, endorsements, and sponsorships, too. Here is a selection of quotes to give you a sense of Djokovic's brand:

"The condemnation was quick, with Australian player Nick Kyrgios labeling it a 'boneheaded decision' to go ahead with the event."
— journalist Danielle Rossingh writing for CNN about the fallout from the Adria Tour, which Djokovic organized during the COVID-19 pandemic and which resulted in several cases of COVID-19 among players, coaches, and families[19]

"You can see that he cares about the sport and you can see that he's trying to do everything he can, from his point of view, that is going to improve this sport."
— professional tennis player Alexander Zverev, commenting on Djokovic founding the players-only Professional Tennis Players Association (PTPA)[20]

"During Covid, [Djokovic is] trying to divide us further when we should be trying to bring the game together."
— women's tennis legend Martina Navratilova, commenting on Djokovic's PTPA efforts[21]

"I have to pay a great tribute to Rafa and Roger. They are legends of our sport and they are the two most important players that I've ever faced

in my career. They are the reason that I am where I am today."
— Novak Djokovic[22]

"It's part of who, I guess, I am. I don't like doing these things. I'm sorry for sending this kind of message, but we're all human beings and sometimes it's difficult to control your emotions."
— Novak Djokovic on his on-court behavior during a loss at the Tokyo Olympics, in which he was warned by the umpire for smashing and throwing his racket[23]

"[Djokovic] pretty much has won the minds of tennis experts. Hearts? That's something else. Like the hunt for Grand Slam titles, that quest goes on."
— ESPN journalist Peter Bodo[24]

Alright, you've read the quotes. Perhaps you checked out recent headlines and the players' social media accounts. You likely had some impression of these athletes before reading this chapter. Who has the stronger and weaker brand?

Lydia Ko represents a stronger brand. Her messaging is clear and consistent. The attributes she is associated with (hard work, trusting in her process, grit, determination), whether ascending to no. 1 in the world or suffering a disappointing setback, are generally positive. She is a phenom not just in terms of her skill at a young age, but also in her ability to handle the pressure. That is why fellow players, coaches, and even former school principals make public statements about how impressive she is.

Novak Djokovic represents a weaker brand. He is a peerless tennis champion whose sustained success does much of the talking. He has stepped up as a leader in his sport, serving as president of the Association of Tennis Professionals (ATP) Tour's Player Council and founding the PTPA in an attempt to better represent players. He launched the Adria Tour during the COVID-19 pandemic to try to keep professional tennis in the spotlight. He is gracious in victory and defeat to his biggest rivals, Federer and Nadal. However, he is also prone to juvenile fits on the court, such as when he accidentally struck an umpire with a ball at the 2020 US Open. His PTPA was criticized by Nadal and Federer, has divided players, and initially drew criticism for not including any women's tennis players. Through all of these PR missteps, he has often criticized the media for engaging in a witch hunt. His actions are inconsistent; further, while some have positive associations, others have negative associations.

This book is intended to help you develop a strong and compelling athlete brand like that of Ko. To reinforce the good, examine a short case study showcasing how one former SA, Nia Dennis, successfully built her brand.

NIA DENNIS: BUILDING AN ATHLETE BRAND FROM A PROGRAM'S BRAND

Consider University of California, Los Angeles (UCLA), women's gymnastics star Nia Dennis, who has vaulted to viral online fame that would be the envy of many professional athletes in a sport that usually generates attention only every four years. Empowered by a coaching staff that encourages joyful and unique performances, Dennis became an online sensation in 2020 with her enthusiastic and technically perfect performance set to a medley of Beyoncé songs. Celebrities like comedian Steve Harvey, actress Gabrielle Union, and legendary Olympic gymnast Simone Biles are among those who have offered her shout-outs on social media. She was even invited to perform a condensed version of the routine on *The Ellen DeGeneres Show*.

While joy and fun are part of the UCLA gymnastics brand, Dennis aligned her performance with her brand by portraying a majorette in the routine: a nod to her family's annual tradition of attending the Bayou Classic Battle of the Bands in New Orleans. Perhaps most importantly, Dennis's decision to bring more of her personal self to her performances was embraced by UCLA head coach Chris Waller, as he told the *Los Angeles Times*:

> It feels a lot to me like she figured out what was important to her. What launched her relatability and self-confidence was a) being herself, but b) investing in the team. The more she threw herself into the team, the more authentic she got and all of the sudden, she personally blew up. [25]

Note how she has used her sport—her platform—to establish who she is while also investing in the team and impressing her coach, all of which builds her reputation and strengthens her athlete brand.

SEVEN WAYS YOUR BRAND CAN HELP YOU ACHIEVE YOUR GOALS (AND SEVEN WAYS IT CAN HURT)

After exploring the different examples of athlete brands (and athlete brand building), a picture is hopefully developing regarding what an athlete brand really is and how one is built. But before you brainstorm ways brand building can help you achieve your goals, it's important that the stakes are perfectly clear. Your brand can help you achieve your goals and vision for your future. It can also hurt. Here are a few ways how.

Help

1. Increase your value at school, with your coach, and with your future coaches

2. Grow your fan base

3. Generate greater interest from sponsors

4. Increase your influence and impact on issues of importance to you

5. Create a strong connection with alumni of your school, who will be a key part of your network regardless of future profession

6. Establish expertise that is in demand for consulting, teaching, and training opportunities

7. Serve as a "tie breaker" when you are in competition for future opportunities

Hurt

1. Jeopardize trust with your coaches, teammates, and future coaches and teammates

2. Diminish not just your fan base, but the respect of your team and teammates

3. Limit future opportunities, including sponsorships and jobs

4. Turn you into a target for unfair criticism and scorn

5. Add stress, anger, and frustration into your daily life

6. Create a negative perception about your "fit" for future roles

7. Lead colleagues to feel you are undesirable to work with

The reality is that brand mishaps happen all the time. They often happen because individuals aren't being strategic about how they manage their brand. They react to a social media post or to something on the court or to an interviewer's question. Through the exercises in this book, you will learn to strategically design—and then consistently activate (i.e., create habits that are consistent with your brand design)—your brand so that you maximize the "help" while minimizing the "hurt."

EXERCISE FIVE
Ways Brand Building Can Help You Achieve Your Goals

Now it's time to answer: How can brand building help you?

Here, you'll find an expanded version of **Exercise 3** with "How Can Brand Building Help?" added as a third column. In the space provided, answer: How can building a stronger brand help you accomplish your in-college goals? And your post-college goals?

Even if you don't plan on continuing in your sport after college (other than as a hobby), how can building a stronger athlete brand help you accomplish your post-college goals? If you're interviewing for a job with a huge fan of your team five years after graduating, do you think you could leverage your reputation to get a leg up on the competition? Or are skills you developed and exhibited as part of your athlete brand—determination, discipline, overcoming obstacles, and a passion for winning—valuable in your career as an engineer, doctor, or businessperson? Of course they are. A stronger in-college athlete brand can be leveraged to help you achieve many longer-term aspirations.

Take some time and think about how a stronger brand can help you achieve your goals. When you're ready, briefly rewrite the role of sport in your life and your goals, then complete the exercise by answering how brand building can help in college and after.

How Can Brand Building Help
You Achieve Your Goals?

IN COLLEGE

AFTER COLLEGE

How Can Brand Building Help You Achieve Your Goals?

IN COLLEGE

- It can help me build a stronger social media presence and following, increasing the number of fans created.

- It can help me become a more valuable member of the basketball team, highly valued for my contribution and impact.

- It can help me strengthen my network inside and outside the sport.

- If I build a better brand with coaches, professors, and businesspeople, it can help me obtain better internships that lead to better training and future career opportunities.

AFTER COLLEGE

- A stronger athlete brand can lead to a more developed network, more fans, and more support and career opportunities after college.

- I can leverage my social media presence and network to demonstrate that I have talent building brands effectively. This can help me: 1) obtain a job in a related career field, and/ or 2) increase the likelihood that prospective employers will have confidence that I know how to manage social media effectively.

- As an athlete who has had to learn about brand building before my peers, I can use this skill to help get jobs and outperform expectations.

CHAPTER 6

Build Your Brand
Like a Temple

Developing Your Athlete Brand

> **"If you don't know where you are going, you'll end up someplace else."**
>
> —*Yogi Berra,*
> MLB Hall of Fame catcher for the New York Yankees

Your work over the last five chapters built an important foundation. It's essential to know where you are going before you start thinking about building a brand that will motivate others to invest in you. This chapter will harness the work you've done to help you begin the process of designing your athlete brand.

WHY YOUR BRAND MATTERS

Why might Tiger Woods care about the perception that fans and sponsors have of him? The answer is simple. An athlete brand carries meaning and value. The stronger your brand, the greater the affinity among more people, and the more your brand is worth.

Woods was the world's highest-paid athlete for nearly a decade, thanks largely to about $100 million in annual earnings from endorsements, from 2001 to 2009. However, scandals related to marital infidelity led directly to Woods losing more than $20 million in endorsements in 2010 alone, and a run of injuries and poor play continued the downward trend.[26] Only after years of physical and reputational rehab, culminating in his 2019 win at the Masters, was Woods able to climb back into the top 10 among the world's highest-paid athletes, with about $60 million annually from endorsements.[27]

A college student with 100,000 TikTok followers can make more money (i.e., monetize their brand) than somebody without a TikTok account. Two SAs with 100,000 TikTok followers can earn vastly different sums based on what each brand stands for (i.e., the positive and negative associations). However, your brand is worth a lot more than just money. Your brand is essentially your reputation. When coaches think highly of you—because, for example, you have developed a brand built on dependability, positive attitude, great work ethic, and a team-first attitude—that impacts how they treat you. It can impact how much time they invest in coaching you or helping you beyond college. And it will probably impact what they tell scouts and other coaches about you. Because your brand impacts what others think about you, it also impacts how they work with you and what they say about you.

As former Starbucks CEO Howard Schultz put it, "If people believe they share values with a company, they will stay loyal to the brand." [28] The coaches, scouts, peers, professors, employers, fans, and others who believe in what you stand for will stay loyal to you and create opportunities for you.

BUILDING YOUR BRAND

The concept of connecting goals to actions to brand development is certainly not new. In fact, the ancient Greek philosopher Socrates is credited with this expert insight every brand manager should know: "The way to gain good reputation is to endeavor to be what you desire to appear." Socrates earns an A in brand building because he understood that *being* what you desire comes first.

When a company's brand managers seek to build a brand, they start with a vision of what they want the brand to stand for in the minds of the target consumers—the subset of consumers who they believe are the right ones to focus their design and activation efforts on. Just as a lacrosse player would not target basketball fans, Tide would not target consumers interested in a sensitive-skin product for newborns.

The tool brand managers use to detail what they want a brand to be known for is called the "brand essence statement," or BES. The keyword here is "essence." It is the brand manager's "blueprint"—defining what they want the brand to stand for. Many athletes live by the credo "your body is your temple." In the world of branding, your BES is your temple, and the framework to create a BES just so happens to look like one of the ancient Greek temples Socrates might have frequented to discuss reputation management.

Figures 2–4 are examples of completed BESs for three members of the 2019 NCAA Tournament champion UVA men's basketball team: point guard Ty Jerome, shooting guard Kyle Guy, and team manager Grant Kersey. While the elements of each BES are the same, each individual's brand should be unique. Take a moment to look over the elements of each BES and see if their brands start to crystallize in your mind. Notice how each has a different target that then influences the rest of their brand design.

Figure 2. Ty Jerome BES.

NBA

Who is your primary target?

What can you do for the target better than anyone else?
> A high-IQ leader who increases success by finding creative solutions and inspiring the team to perform their best, enabling the coach to trust him to win.

What proof can you provide to demonstrate you can deliver on the benefits above?

SUPERIOR WORK ETHIC	OUTLEARN OTHERS	TEAM LEADER
Committed to outworking anyone and everyone	Committed to learning about the craft of basketball to enable better performance	Earns the respect of his teammates through his dedication to helping others perform their best

How do you operate? How do others describe you? What are your personality traits?

Dependable   Gritty Competitor   Authentic New York   Winner

It is important to note the difference between a brand purpose and a professional brand's target audience. Jerome's brand purpose and "who he does it for" are his family and close friends, while his professional target audience is the NBA. The NBA level of basketball is what he has been working toward his entire life and is therefore what makes up his target audience.

Figure 3. Kyle Guy BES.

FANS

Who is your primary target?

What can you do for the target better than anyone else?
> An especially exceptional NBA player who inspires the next generation of athletes by engaging with fans through exclusive, personal "inside basketball" stories and content.

What proof can you provide to demonstrate you can deliver on the benefits above?

Consistently interacts with fans via Twitter, Instagram, Facebook, etc.	Posts content on basketball, his time at UVA, interests off the court, and other aspects of his life.	Supports key causes such as mental health awareness, veteran support, clean water, and much more.	Strives to behave in a way that is aspirational to young fans.

How do you operate? How do others describe you? What are your personality traits?

Giver   Genuine   Down-to-Earth

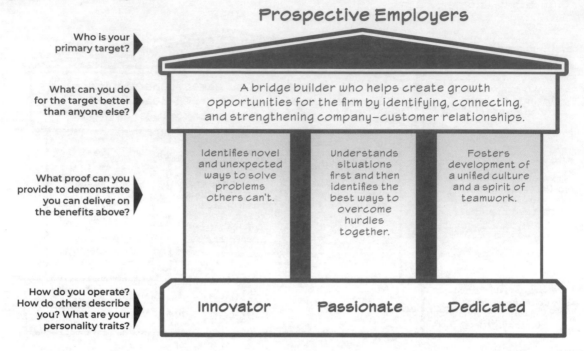

Figure 4. Grant Kersey BES.

Who is your primary target?

What can you do for the target better than anyone else?

What proof can you provide to demonstrate you can deliver on the benefits above?

How do you operate? How do others describe you? What are your personality traits?

Prospective Employers

A bridge builder who helps create growth opportunities for the firm by identifying, connecting, and strengthening company–customer relationships.

Identifies novel and unexpected ways to solve problems others can't.

Understands situations first and then identifies the best ways to overcome hurdles together.

Fosters development of a unified culture and a spirit of teamwork.

Innovator   Passionate   Dedicated

THE FOUR KEY SECTIONS OF THE BRAND ESSENCE STATEMENT

As you can see in the examples, there are four key elements of the BES.

1. Target

Who is the most important primary target for you? If you plan to be a professional athlete or Olympian, it may very well be coaches and scouts. If you don't plan to play past college, your target may ultimately be prospective employers. You might have goals that require you to significantly grow your public image, which means your target might be fans. The idea is to identify your core target audience in the BES.

As an example of how this works, consider Tide laundry detergent. Tide primarily targets parents with kids.

Why? Because that is who consumes the most laundry detergent. Does Tide want other people to buy the product? Sure. But Tide designs its brand to target the most important group.

Likewise, SAs care about what professors, coaches, fans, and others think, but it is important for each SA to figure out the central, most important target.

Key Target Questions to Ask

- Who matters most as you develop your brand—college coaches, professors, scouts and professional coaches, fans, or another group? This is your primary target.

- Why is this your primary target? Your answer should be closely aligned with your goals and vision for your future.

2. Benefit

This section should reflect the value that you want to create for your target. Tide's benefit is to provide superior performance on the toughest of laundry problems. Coca-Cola's benefit is to provide uplifting refreshment. Verizon's benefit is to provide the best network coverage, wherever you go. Brands must provide some meaningful value for their target in order to be appealing. To repurpose the famous quote from President John F. Kennedy, "Ask not what your target can do for you but what you can do for your target."

In the context of an athlete, consider Jerome's benefit. His goals as a college athlete were to win an NCAA national championship and get to the NBA. He cared about developing an athlete brand that his UVA coaches, NBA scouts, and NBA coaches would respect and desire. Interestingly, the benefit he provided was being, in short, a "winner." He was a tough, gritty competitor who didn't let any limitation hold him back. In high school, he had double hip surgery his senior year. He also was consistently told throughout his life that he wasn't "athletic enough." None of that mattered. His brand was about finding a way to win through hard work, unmatched competitive will, and high mental aptitude for the game.

Key Benefit Questions to Ask

- What do you think your target wants (i.e., what makes an "exceptional brand" for these individuals)?

- What do you do differently/better than everybody else? What is your "superpower"? What have peers and coaches told you are your greatest strengths and greatest value you bring to the team?

- What benefit do you provide for your target? How can you create value for your target?

3. Reasons to Believe

Tide can say that it delivers great performance on important laundry problems, but why should you believe it? Jerome can say that he is a gritty winner, but where is his proof to make coaches believe it? The reasons to believe are the supporting evidence that enables your target to believe your benefit. Verizon has claimed for years that it has the "best" network coverage. How does Verizon prove it? It shows you a map of its coverage relative to competitors.

In this section, you want to think about how you will prove that you can deliver the benefit. Looking at Jerome's example again, notice that he focused on three areas to help ensure he could become a "winner": (1) superior work ethic, (2) "outlearning" others, and (3) being a team leader.

Key Reasons to Believe Questions to Ask

- What support can you provide that demonstrates your superpower? Any numbers? Facts? Press clippings?

- What have peers and coaches told you are the specific ways in which you deliver your superpower?

4. Personality

The final section of the BES is the brand personality. This section details the personality characteristics that distinguish you from others. If Tide were a person, who would it be and why? Perhaps a friendly, caring, and knowledgeable neighbor who is always there when you need them? If you think about the personalities of Conor McGregor or Naomi Osaka or Kyrie Irving or Megan Rapinoe, what comes to mind?

You want to be clear about your brand personality and pick distinctive words. In Jerome's example, the words he used to describe himself were "gritty," "dependable," and "New York." These words took time to choose because he wanted adjectives that were accurate and also captured dimensions of

difference. "Gritty" and "New York" help paint a clearer picture of the type of person he is than "hardworking" and "tough," which are more generic. The more precise and descriptive you can be, the better.

Key Personality Questions to Ask

- How do others describe you?

- What descriptors (i.e., adjectives) are most identifying and unique to you?

GET TO KNOW YOUR BRAND: DO YOUR RESEARCH

How can you figure out what your current brand is? A starting point is to do a little research by asking those who know you best. Before you go any further, look for insight in four areas: 1) your coaches and mentors, 2) other SAs who are on your team or with whom you compete, 3) close family and friends, and 4) your interviews, press conferences, and media appearances.

Identify 5 to 10 people from the above areas to answer the following questions. You can interview them (which may take more time) or ask them the questions via email to get the answers in writing.

1. How would you describe (your name) in general?

2. What distinguishing attributes does (your name) bring as an athlete?

3. How would you describe (your name)'s personality?

Finally, review any taped media appearances or quotes from your interviews that have appeared in print.

After retrieving this information, assemble it all in one place (e.g., a Word document or in PowerPoint). Are there any patterns or trends? What common themes emerge? You are triangulating across different people and perspectives to try to identify the "brand you are." This is the starting point in designing the brand you want to become. If you need a little more guidance, Rebecca Jarrett's answers to the questions, her completed BES, and a "brand board" are available after the exercise. In her brand board,

Jarrett summarizes information from different perspectives to identify trends and patterns that helped her develop her BES.

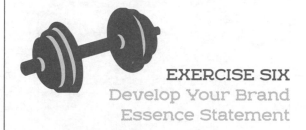

EXERCISE SIX
Develop Your Brand
Essence Statement

Now that you've learned more about the four key elements of the BES, examined a few completed BES pyramids, and have a good sense of your current brand, you're ready to design your desired brand. Answer the following questions. A hint: As you work through this, continue to talk to people who know you best if you need additional insight and perspective.

1. Who matters most as you develop your brand (current coaches, professors, professional scouts and coaches, fans, future employer, etc.)? This is your primary target.

TARGET

3. What support can you provide that demonstrates you have this superpower? Any numbers? Facts? Evidence? Proof?

REASONS TO BELIEVE (3–4)

2. What benefit do you provide your target? What is your "superpower"?

BENEFIT

4. How do others describe you? What descriptors are most identifying and unique to you?

PERSONALITY

Now that you've answered these questions, convert your answers into a summary BES template. This will enable you to share your BES with mentors, advisers, parents, and others to get feedback and better refine it.

Who is your primary target? ▶

What can you do for the target better than anyone else? ▶

What proof can you provide to demonstrate you can deliver on the benefits above? ▶

How do you operate? How do others describe you? What are your personality traits? ▶

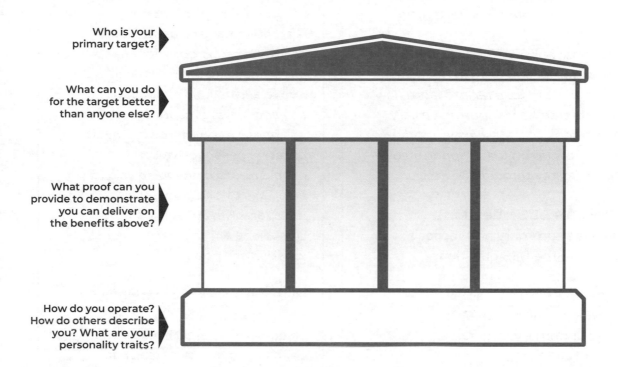

REBECCA JARRETT'S COMPLETED EXERCISE

Rebecca's current brand

Below are a sample of quotes and insight she received from coaches, peers, family, and friends. While she received many more, this provides you with an idea of the type of feedback you should seek to receive.

"Rebecca is one of the finest student-athletes I have ever had the pleasure of coaching in my time in college athletics. She is a special individual who is constantly looking for ways to grow as a person, student, athlete, and leader."

"I have witnessed many SAs come to Virginia and not take advantage of the world-class institution that it is...not Rebecca. She is squeezing absolutely everything out of her education that she can and inspiring others along the way."

"I think you have a very engaging personality—you are warm, honest, welcoming, and have a gregarious personality. You do a very good job of bringing people together— inviting, inclusive, and I think people want to be around you as a result."

"Responsiveness to feedback, coachability, and growth mindset. Willingness to take risks to learn new skills, create new opportunities, try new things, etc. Most importantly, you follow up on these opportunities! Again, follow-through! Reliability!"

Rebecca's BES questions

Below is a summary of Rebecca's answers to the BES questions.

1. Who matters most as you develop your brand? This is your primary target.

TARGET

Future employers and my growing professional network. My goal is to leverage my soccer experience when applicable to strengthen my network and demonstrate my commitment to excellence— both of which should help me land professional opportunities.

2. What benefit do you provide your target? What is your superpower?

BENEFIT

I believe that my target audience (primarily prospective employers) would want someone who is committed to excellence, works hard, has a great attitude, and is trustworthy and dependable. I demonstrate a commitment to excellence by consistently going above and beyond expectations to "wow" my professors, coaches, and bosses. I do this by bringing a creative perspective to problems and developing unique solutions to challenges. I also bring a "never-give-up" spirit to the workplace and try to always be uplifting and positive.

My superpower is creating solutions that provide unique insight and thinking on tough problems in a way that strengthens the team and workplace. I am a hyper-visual thinker who sees the world in a unique way; therefore, my superpower is how I think through problems in a way that creates unique solutions and strengthens the team/workplace.

3. What support can you provide that demonstrates you have this superpower? Any numbers? Facts?

REASONS TO BELIEVE

My coaches and bosses have gone out of their way to nominate me for scholarships and awards or write me letters of recommendation with high praise. For example, my head coach, Steve Swanson, wrote in a nomination letter: *"Rebecca is one of the finest student-athletes I have ever had the pleasure of coaching in my time in college athletics. She is a special individual who is constantly looking for ways to grow as a person, student, athlete and leader."* He then went on to say: *"I have known Rebecca for over four years in my capacity as women's soccer coach at the University of Virginia and feel strongly, given her extraordinary service to our soccer program, her commitment to excellence in the classroom, her leadership skills, her service to the community, and her incredible enthusiasm for the University of Virginia and life in general that she is an outstanding candidate for the T. Rodney Crowley Scholarship Award."*

Articles that have appeared on virginiasports.com and in the local Charlottesville paper suggest that I am uniquely well-rounded. For example, journalist Caron Merk wrote: *"Rebecca Jarrett is a star on the University of Virginia's women's soccer team. But, she's equally impressive off the pitch with her thoughtfulness, intelligence, and talent"* (via Beautiful Game Network).

4. How do others describe you? What descriptors are most identifying and unique to you?

PERSONALITY

I asked some of the people I interact with most (including teammates, close friends, and coaches) to describe me and sourced news articles about myself to identify what descriptors are most commonly associated with me.

A close friend and fellow UVA student-athlete said, *"You always put others first and support your friends to the end of the world and back."*

One of my assistant coaches said, *"I think you have a very engaging personality. You are warm, honest, welcoming, and have a gregarious personality. You do a very good job of bringing people together—inviting, inclusive, and I think people want to be around you as a result."* He also commended me for *"[my] work ethic and the fact [that I] willingly seek out challenges."* Lastly, he said, *"I think this quality transcends multiple aspects of your life during your time here at Virginia. First, in regard to soccer, the qualitative improvements as a player that have taken place are in no small part a result of your receptiveness to coaching, but more importantly, your willingness to work on different aspects of your game has helped you become an impactful player at the highest level of college soccer. Academically, you do well in the classroom, but you make a point of seeking opportunities to challenge yourself in other ways. And finally, your engagement socially and the way in which you have sought a deeper understanding and pushed others to challenge their perspectives on social justice issues is not easy nor something most people are willing to engage."*

Rebecca's BES

Rebecca then translated her answers into the simple visual in **Figure 5**. While she is focused on athletics for the next several years, she wanted to think about a longer-term view of her brand...what it will be after athletics. Consequently, she created her brand with a future career in business in mind.

Figure 5. Rebecca Jarrett's BES.

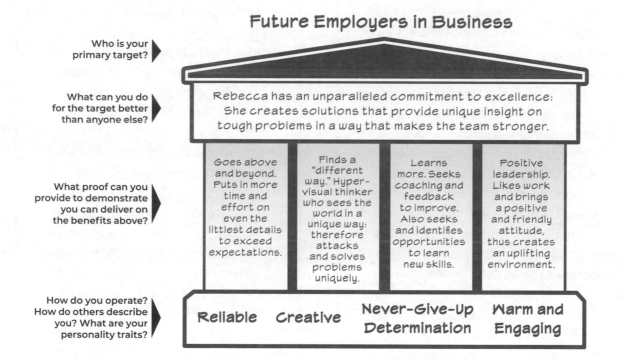

EXTRA CREDIT
Creative Ways to Develop a More Complete Brand Picture: Creating a Brand Board

Rebecca has a list of credentials a mile long, including being named to the College Cup All-Tournament team, the All-ACC second team, and the ACC Championship All-Tournament team. As she worked on this exercise, she created a "brand essence idea board" **(Figure 6)** on which she included her thoughts and quotes from coaches, family, and friends.

What is a brand essence idea board? It's much like any idea board, often in the form of a one-page summary that allows you to quickly show and explain what the brand is. The board might include photos, quotes from others, brand traits and benefits—anything that succinctly and effectively conveys the brand's essence. You can create a board as an incremental step before completing your BES.

Not only was creating a board a creative way to integrate Rebecca's own perspective with insight from others, but it was also useful in helping her develop a more complete picture of her superpower. Of note, Rebecca did this on her own, without any guidance. Can you see how she demonstrated her "superpower" (hyper-visual thinker who sees the world in a unique way) through her brand essence idea board?

Figure 6. Rebecca Jarrett's brand essence idea board.

target	benefit	reasons to believe
who? Future employers My growing professional network	Employers (my primary target) want someone who consistently delivers high quality results, has unique insights, and a positive attitude	- excels on the field and in the classroom - has a positive, growth mindset - goes above and beyond what is expected - takes risks and tries new things - learns more, thus delivers better results - has an inviting and friendly leadership style

why?
One of my main goals is to leverage my soccer experience, and opportunities I have gained through that experience, to help me market myself as the "quintessential student-athlete" to my target.

Quotes from coaches, peers, and press clippings:

Quotes from my head coach:

excels on the field and in the classroom

"I have known Rebecca for over four years in my capacity as women's soccer coach at the University of Virginia and feel strongly, given her extraordinary service to our soccer program, her commitment to excellence in the classroom, her leadership skills, her service to the community, and her incredible enthusiasm for the University of Virginia and life in general that she is an outstanding candidate for the *** Award."

growth mindset

"Rebecca is one of the finest student athletes I have ever had the pleasure of coaching in my time in college athletics. She is a special individual who is constantly is looking for ways to grow as a person, student, athlete and leader."

goes above and beyond what is expected

"I have witnessed many student-athletes come to Virginia and not take advantage of the world class institution that it is...not Rebecca. She is squeezing absolutely everything out of her education that she can and inspiring others along the way."

positive risk-taker

"Responsiveness to feedback, coachability, and growth mindset. Willingness to take risks to learn new skills, create new opportunities, try new things, etc. Most importantly: you follow up on these opportunities! Again, Follow Through! (Reliability)"
-Academic Coordinator

tries new things = learns more, thus delivers better results

"You do a great job of taking an unbiased stance on serious situations which makes you very reliable. You're so incredibly smart and that speaks for itself. Anything you get involved in you immerse yourself wholeheartedly. You never do anything half-assed."
-Best Friend

"Rebecca Jarrett is a star on the University of Virginia's women's soccer team. But, she's equally impressive off the pitch with her thoughtfulness, intelligence, and talent."
- Carson Merk, bgm.fm

well-rounded

friendly leadership style

"I think you have a very engaging personality - you are warm, honest, welcoming, and a have a gregarious personality. You do a very good job of bringing people together - inviting, inclusive and I think people want to be around you as a result."
-Assistant Coach

CHAPTER 7

Easier Said
Than Done

Setting Your Brand Boundaries

> **" Be more concerned with your character than your reputation. Because your character is what you really are, while your reputation is merely what others think you are. "**
>
> *—John Wooden,*
>
> 10-time NCAA men's basketball championship–winning head coach of the UCLA Bruins

You've started to design your brand. Congratulations!

Before moving ahead to brand activation, there are two important issues you should consider because of the outsized impact they will have on your ability to actually achieve the brand you desire.

First, you'll need to decide on your brand boundaries: the guardrails that will help ensure that you engage in activities that strengthen (versus weaken) your brand.

SETTING YOUR BRAND BOUNDARIES

One thing that can happen, especially with "professional" brands (as opposed to product-based brands), is that it is hard to behave in alignment with your desired brand strategy every minute of the day. Many celebrities have fallen prey to the single statement or single action that derails their brand.

Consider Andre Gray, the soccer player who achieved his dream of playing in the English Premier League in 2016, until homophobic tweets he wrote in 2012 surfaced. At a time when he should have been celebrating reaching the pinnacle of his sport, his team released him and he was sanctioned by the league's governing body.[29]

Professional marketers also make mistakes when working on product-based brands. Consider Gillette's "Toxic Masculinity" advertisement. In the midst of the #MeToo movement, the brand sought to take a stand and convince men—Gillette's primary consumers—to behave better. The reaction to the campaign was swift, much of it negative.

University of Dayton communication professor Alan Abitbol wrote in *The Conversation* that Gillette's ad "missed the mark" because the cause (ending toxic masculinity) was not connected in a clear way to the brand, which made many feel the ad was inauthentic.[30] Nearly everyone would agree that men behaving in caring and respectful ways is a good thing. However, when the target audience doesn't see a clear connection between a brand and its message, the audience is often left confused and angry, wondering why the brand is delivering that message. The consequence is a target audience that now believes the brand is opportunistic or views it with skepticism.

If even professionals have difficulty, how can you, as an SA, grow your brand in a way that protects it from mistakes that weaken both your brand image and brand value?

ESTABLISH GUARDRAILS THAT ENABLE YOU TO MINIMIZE RISKS

You want to create discipline by constructing boundaries that identify which activities are "in the fairway" and which are "out of bounds." This helps you think ahead about what is "on strategy" (or consistent with your desired brand) and what isn't. With this comes guardrails: strategic decisions set in place to keep you from straying out of bounds. These will vary with your chosen brand image, but basic guardrails will typically include the followng:

1. Don't post or publicly comment on hot-button issues (politics, religion, and so on)

2. Don't post or publicly comment if judgment is impaired (such as if tired, angry, or drinking alcoholic beverages)

3. Stay positive as much as possible (focus on identifying the good and not the bad)

4. Don't get baited into arguing, defending, or debating

5. Stay disciplined and only post or publicly comment on topics related to content strategy

6. Practice the golden rule of social media: when in doubt, ignore

THREE REASONS TO STAY INSIDE YOUR GUARDRAILS WITH "OFF BRAND" ISSUES YOU CARE ABOUT

Given the suggested guardrails, an interesting question could be: Why not use the platform to have positive impact on a topic that is important to you but may be quite controversial?

This is a terrific question and one deserving of a nuanced answer. It comes down to this: If you use your resources (the most precious one being time) to wade outside of the boundaries you have established, you reduce your resources available to fulfill the primary goals you set at the beginning of this process. Further, you may inadvertently shrink the audience of people interested in following you when you veer off topic. Worse, you may unintentionally develop your brand in a way that turns off your target. If you are interested in getting to the pros or getting hired by a company, then your target—the people who will hire you—may use your public statements to better understand your brand and whether it fits with their organization's brand.

Reason No. 1

As the above suggests, it's critical to stay focused on—and not detract from—your primary goal. The more different topics you talk about, the more confused your brand can become. To illustrate, think of an SA who wants to get to the Olympics. Their short-term mission is to excel at their sport so that they can reach the pinnacle. Any significant investment in activities outside of this mission potentially impacts their ability to achieve their Olympic dream and

could impact what their target thinks of them (i.e., their brand image).

Reason No. 2

There is another way to think about using your platform: when should you use your platform to have additional impact beyond your primary purpose. If you read everything about what then–NBA rookie Zion Williamson said near the start of the COVID-19 pandemic, during great political divisions, and while people were marching across the United States following the murder of George Floyd, you might be surprised.

What did Williamson say about all of these issues? Not much. Why? Did he not care? Could it be because he was still in the infancy of building his brand and it was not the right time to veer away from basketball and possibly alienate fans, which would reduce his brand value and potentially risk income, sponsorships, and his ability to make a bigger impact in the future? By staying inside his guardrails early in his career, Williamson is building a bigger and stronger brand, which he can (and likely will) use to make a larger impact later. While this may seem frustrating, it is a strategic approach to brand building.

Reason No. 3

You can have an impact in ways other than posting on social media. For example, although Kim generally follows the above guardrails in social media, she tries to make a difference at a more personal level by: speaking at and mentoring several individuals from underrepresented demographic groups. Every time she walks into class, the more competent she is, the better she represents female leaders. That also has an impact on how young people view women.

There is a push most SAs feel right now to use their platforms to make statements on what are often highly polarizing and divisive issues. Have you noticed that the people often pushing SAs to use their platforms either aren't doing it themselves or don't have as much to lose? Short-term decisions to engage on divisive issues publicly can have long-term consequences for your brand and, more importantly, your ability to achieve your goals. It can feel good to fire off a tweet to somebody who said something on the other side of an issue you care about. However, the consequences may be more tangible and longer lasting than you want.

Think about the goals you have, the brand you want to achieve, and the guardrails you want to construct to minimize the risk and maximize your ability to achieve your dreams. This is an individual decision: only you can identify the right boundaries to help you achieve your short- and long-term goals.

APPLYING BRAND BOUNDARIES TO YOUR LIFE AS AN SA

As an SA with an athlete brand, public comments and stances on controversial topics will impact your audience. Those who agree may like it. Those who don't may not. And then there are some who watch you only because of your athletic prowess, and who will tune out because they no longer find you entertaining.

According to Sprout Social's 2019 Brands Get Real report,[31] "55% of consumers say they would boycott or discontinue shopping with brands that support public issues that don't align with their own views. And 34% of consumers would decrease their spending with a brand whose stances they disagree with." A 2020 Harris Poll sought to unearth why NBA TV ratings suffered a precipitous drop after returning from its COVID-19 break in play, only to discover that 38% of respondents said they stopped watching because "the league has become too political." [32] The NBA and its players, of course, had taken a prominent stance in support of social justice issues during a summer of unrest following the murder of George Floyd.

On the flip side, there certainly can be a positive case for building brand value through taking a stand on an issue. A 2018 Edelman Earned Brand report[33] found that 64% of consumers are "belief-driven buyers," more than two-thirds of whom reported buying a brand for the first time because of its position on a controversial issue and 65% of whom reported not buying a brand because it stayed silent on an issue they felt it had an obligation to address. When brands do take a stand with which consumers align, 36% say they'll purchase more from that company, according to the Sprout Social report.

If it feels like a "damned if you do, damned if you don't" situation, you're not alone. That's why it's important that, if you take a stand on a controversial or polarizing issue, it be meaningful to you, aligned with your goals and vision, and carefully integrated into your brand. Further, you should ponder how this will impact your brand over the long term, making sure you are aware of the consequences and comfortable with the potential outcome before taking a stand. This may also include asking your coaches and other key stakeholders for their opinions.

Unfortunately, many who engage in controversial topics do so because they don't have a brand strategy. They have likely failed to identify what they want their brand to be or to stay disciplined in activating the brand. Instead, they inadvertently say something on social media, in the heat of the moment, or do something that can have undesirable consequences. Your brand can impact whether you are drafted, whether sponsors want to work with you, and many other playing and financial opportunities. Because of the very significant personal consequences, many athletes don't engage in controversial topics until they are financially set and are more comfortable shouldering any negative press. Of course, taking a stand on issues that aren't polarizing (e.g., body image, mental health, etc.) doesn't carry the same risk.

However, each person must decide how to build and manage their own brand. Make a strategic decision regarding the boundaries you wish to set for your own brand.

BRAND BOUNDARIES AND THE MEDIA

Many SAs will be interviewed by the media at some point during their careers. Interviews present a great opportunity to strengthen your brand, but they also pose a significant risk if you are unprepared. After all, the media's job is to write stories that interest readers and generate clicks or subscriptions. What achieves a reporter's goal—such as commenting on the latest controversy in the news—might not help you achieve your goals. Check the sports headlines for a week and count how many times professional athletes spend the next day backtracking after offering off-the-cuff responses to reporters' questions about the controversy du jour. Unfortunately, you'll find several.

Before accepting interviews outside the usual post-game or regularly scheduled press conference routine, you should check with your school's athletic communications office. As you'll learn in the next chapter, it's crucial that your brand be aligned with your school and your program. Most athletic departments will help to coordinate the interview, unearth topics of interest for the reporter ahead of time, and ensure any necessary precautions are taken.

Your athletic department might provide media training for athletes, but here are a few quick pointers:

- **Be confident and cool.** You are the subject-matter expert. Your thoughts and opinions are valued and wanted.

- **Prepare mentally.** Take a minute before the interview to catch your breath and switch your mindset from game to media. Emotional post-game responses can be damaging to your brand.

- **Think fast, talk slow.** Take your time to give an articulate and thoughtful response.

- **Avoid conflict.** Don't speak negatively about others and don't feel like you must answer every question. If you're not comfortable with the question, a simple "I'm not going to talk about that" or "I don't have an answer for that" will suffice. Avoid saying "no comment," as audiences have learned to infer negative or deeper meaning in the statement. As you become more sophisticated, you will learn to "block and pivot." In other words, if they ask a question you don't want to answer, you don't respond and essentially answer a different question.

- **Be concise.** Rambling only increases your chances of being misquoted or otherwise hurting your brand.

- **Be "on brand."** Think about the BES you created in the last chapter. How can you answer questions in a way that reinforces your brand?

Regarding the last point, consider UVA men's basketball head coach Tony Bennett. If you watch his interviews over time, you'll see that almost all his comments reinforce his "Five Pillars" (thankfulness, servanthood, humility, passion, and unity). He references these over and over and over again—to the point where, as a fan, you can't help but know what he stands for. Consistency and repetition is critical in developing your brand.

Leveraging media interviews to help establish and solidify your brand is wise. But you must think ahead about how you will do that.

In addition to your school's media training, you may choose to take a class or read any number of free articles online. Your brand and future self will thank you!

QUESTIONS TO ANSWER BEFORE ENGAGING IN CONTROVERSIAL OR POLARIZING ISSUES

Do you want to engage in controversial topics publicly? If so, how? Which topics? And when is optimal—in college, after you've landed your first professional contract, or after you've made millions and are financially set for life? Most importantly, what are the consequences, and are you comfortable with the potential outcomes?

If an important issue motivates you, taking a stance and using your athlete brand platform can be an incredible way to make a positive difference in the world. Before engaging, however, ask yourself the following questions:

1. Is your engagement on the issue consistent with your brand strategy?

2. Will it strengthen your brand image and help you achieve your goals?

3. Do most people agree with your position or is there division and dissent? Former NFL defensive end Chris Long founded Waterboys during his playing career to provide sustainable access to clean drinking water for 1 million people worldwide. Many issues critical to the well-being of society are contentious, but you'd be hard-pressed to find anyone who doesn't support universal access to clean water. The risk associated with an issue that almost everybody supports is far lower than picking something aligned with, say, a political party, which is inherently controversial and divisive.

4. Is the position you choose to support also supported by most of your target audience? For example, if your target audience is professional coaches, would they generally support or agree with you becoming vocal on the issue? If your target happens to be your current coach, would he or she think your public engagement is positive for your team and university? If fans are your target, would they agree with your position?

5. If your target doesn't fully align with the position you want to advocate for, what are the potential consequences? How many fans might you lose? What would your coach think (a suggestion: talk to your coach first and find out)? What might professional coaches think? What could happen to your brand image and potential profit?

6. Are you comfortable with the potential ramifications of your decision?

EXERCISE SEVEN
Define Your Guardrails

Here, identify the guardrails that you want to erect to grow and protect your brand.

To help you brainstorm, here are the guardrails Grant Kersey set during his time as a team manager and walk-on player for the UVA men's basketball team.

GRANT KERSEY'S COMPLETED EXERCISE

- Keep content team centered.

- Always act within the Five Pillars (Coach Tony Bennett's program-defining principles).

- Always stay positive.

- Do not over-post or post too often.

- Golden rule: If you doubt it, do not do it.

1.

2.

3.

4.

5.

6.

7.

8.

9.

10.

CHAPTER 8

Your Brand Does Not Live in a Vacuum

How to Integrate Your Brand with Other Brands

> **“ Individual commitment to a group effort—that is what makes a team work, a company work, a society work, a civilization work. ”**
>
> *—Vince Lombardi,*
> two-time Super Bowl–winning, NFL Hall of Fame coach of the Green Bay Packers

Now that you have developed the guardrails that will help protect your brand, it's time to think about how your brand interacts with your team's brand and that of your school.

To understand the interaction, consider the New England Patriots. The brand of the New England Patriots throughout the era led by quarterback Tom Brady and head coach Bill Belichick was centered on the mantra: "Do your job." The organization's brand was hyper-focused on winning and the process to achieve those wins. Every player was expected to buy in to "the Patriot way." Behaviors drawing attention to individuals or providing juicy sound bites to the media were discouraged. The organization embraced an identity as a winning machine where the parts (the players) other than Brady and Belichick were interchangeable.

Players looking to rehabilitate their careers after personal or professional issues, such as Randy Moss and Antonio Brown, joined the team to prove they could fit in and contribute to the winning recipe.

Does that sound like a suitable landing spot for a free spirit who likes to talk to the media, engage on social media, and live in the spotlight? Not particularly.

Similarly, your college team and university have brands. These brands are based on their principles and values but can also be shaped by reputations and stereotypes over which they have little control.

As mentioned before, Coach Tony Bennett's Virginia Cavaliers are built on the Five Pillars of humility, passion, unity, servanthood, and thankfulness. Players are expected to embrace those pillars, which in turn helps define their brand. When commentators started to negatively shape the brand by calling Virginia's playing style "slow and boring," the program worked to flip the script on this criticism by adopting "Embrace the Pace" as an ethos that tied Virginia's style to winning.

In other example, John Calipari's Kentucky Wildcats are often the one-year landing pad for top NBA prospects, and thus the program is known as a star showcase for individual skills.

Not only do these program brands help define the players' brands, but the players have an obligation to represent their program's brand by virtue of joining the team that is the best fit.

Former UVA men's basketball player Anthony Gill is a perfect case in point of matching personal brand to program brand. He embraced UVA's Five Pillars when he transferred to UVA from South Carolina, and he carried the pillars forward as part of his brand into his professional career; he spent several years in the EuroLeague before finally getting an opportunity in the NBA with the Washington Wizards.

For the first two-thirds of his first NBA season, Gill was buried at the end of the bench, where you couldn't blame a player for being less than fully engaged. In the final third of the 2020–21 season, however, Gill earned

a crucial role as the Wizards made a surprise run to clinch a playoff spot. When asked why he started playing Gill, Wizards coach Scott Brooks said, "The guy works harder than anybody on our team. He comes in every day. He comes in early. He's always cheering his teammates on, he's the first one up [off the bench]." After Gill's first breakout performance, all-star point guard Russell Westbrook said Gill "does all the right things" so "you want to make sure guys like that get rewarded." [34]

Your university's brand likely presents a similar dynamic. For example, UVA has a distinct brand centered around academic prestige, honor, and student leadership. Notre Dame's brand is closely tied to the practice of Roman Catholicism and Irish Catholic culture. Eureka College, a small liberal arts college in Illinois, which competes in Division III and is the alma mater of former President Ronald Reagan, was founded by abolitionists and maintains strong ties to its founding purpose to provide a values- and service-driven educational experience. Expectations of you held by university stakeholders like alumni, donors, faculty, and the administration will differ based on the university, and this *should* influence your brand and your behavior.

From the university's perspective, a scholarship is a form of payment. For some, it provides a free education. If you are aspiring to play at the next level, the university provides a platform enabling you to be developed, coached, and seen by top professional recruiters. The school can also provide media exposure. Simply, the school helps you and you help the school. It is not a one-way street. When you are being compensated, there is an assumption that you will act in support of and in concert with the brand of the company that employs you (or university and program that provides your scholarship and opportunity to compete). In the new NIL world, your school may also provide you with access to wealthy alumni and supporters who will connect you with money-making opportunities.

The brand of your team and university can have "spillover" effects, both positive and negative. This is when brand attributes of one brand spill over and impact another brand. For example, if you play on a team that is found to have cheated, this can have a potential spillover effect on your brand.

Figure 7. Brand spillover.

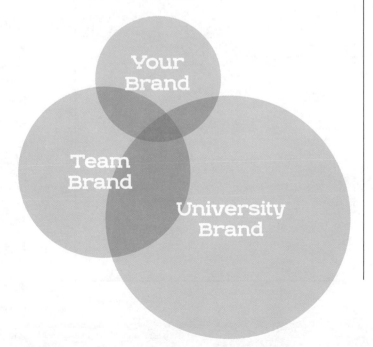

If an SA engages in illegal or criminal behavior—or simply tweets something that is inconsistent with the team's and university's brands—this can spill over onto their brands. All these brands, to a certain extent, are bound together and overlap, as shown in the diagram in **Figure 7**.

EXERCISE EIGHT
Understanding Multilevel Brand Integration

How does your brand support your team and university brands? To understand the answer to that question, you'll need to first think about your team's and school's brands. Describe your team's brand and your university's brand, then think about how your brand and those brands can mutually support and strengthen each other.

You will see an example of how Rebecca Jarrett defined UVA women's soccer's brand and UVA's brand. What do you notice? There is a theme across all three brands (Rebecca, UVA, UVA women's soccer) about a competitive spirit that is understated and humble but strives for perfection. The "great and good" concept—great performers who also do good for others—is common to all three brands.

1. Describe your team's brand.

3. Describe your university's brand.

2. As you develop your brand, how can you help support and strengthen your team's and university's brands?

4. How might your team's and university's brands help support and strengthen your brand?

REBECCA JARRET'S COMPLETED EXERCISE

Women's Soccer Team's Brand

"All in" culture

Great players AND great people

Not cocky or flashy

Hardworking and humble

Rebecca's Brand (from her BES)

Goes above and beyond

Finds a "different way"

Learns more

Positive leadership

UVA's Brand

"Great and good"

Elite and prestigious university

Ultra-competitive

Honor

CHAPTER 9

Getting in the Game

Activating Your Brand

> " Vision without action is merely a dream. Action without vision just passes the time. Vision with action can change the world. "

—Joel Barkeri,

futurist, filmmaker, and author

Y ou are purposely developing a vision, goals, brand strategy, and plans to implement the strategy. But having a vision on paper is the easy part. The harder part is staying disciplined in delivering that vision. When a tweet inflames you, how do you make sure not to respond if it doesn't serve your brand? Or if an interviewer asks you an offensive question, how do you respond in a way that supports your brand?

Thus far, you have spent a lot of time thinking about your future and the type of brand you want to create to help you achieve your athletic goals. This is akin to watching a lot of tape on competitors or listening to coaches talk about plans for a game. It's time for you to "get in the game" and to start to think about how you will implement your brand— what we like to call brand activation.

HOW BRAND ACTIVATION WORKS

A brand activation plan is the summary of the specific choices you are making to consistently deliver the brand promise across all touchpoints. In other words, you develop a plan that identifies how you will behave to advance your brand strategy. Ty Jerome called this process "habit-shifting." To deliver your brand, you must create habits that support the design.

Look at Coach Tony Bennett, who is known for his "pack line" defense. His teams tend to be methodical, smart, and strategic. On offense, they pass up good shots to find the best shot. On defense, they take pride in being so tough that they create shot clock violations. This "brand" of basketball results in fewer possessions per game and a slower style of play. While Bennett may communicate the strategy, he must come up practice sessions that make these plans concrete and game plans that activate his vision. And then the basketball team has to play in accordance with the game plan.

This helps explain the importance of brand activation. It converts strategy into a game plan that the brand (in this case, you) must consistently deliver.

BRINGING A BRAND TO LIFE

Now that you have a good sense of Ty Jerome's brand, what do you think he would be like? What might somebody say about him? Consider the following excerpts from the first and last paragraphs of *The Athletic*'s January 2019 article[35] about Jerome. How does this map onto his brand strategy? When a reporter says this about him, do you think his habits helped deliver his desired brand?

He can't even remember what the argument was over. Something minor, of that he's certain. All Ty Jerome knows is he needed to be right, to be vindicated and above all else, to win. This is how he is wired— you play to win. Win games, win drills, and yes, win arguments, which is why, on that recent afternoon in the Virginia weight room, he kept going. "Snapping and snapping and snapping," is how he remembers

it, until strength and conditioning coach Mike Curtis finally pulled him aside and told him enough.

Which is why, at the end of practice, as everyone else filters out the door, Ty stands at a side hoop and shoots. He started the ritual years ago, setting a goal to knock down 9 of 10 3-pointers before hitting the showers. There have been days it has taken 30 minutes and times when he's had to go in for a film session before returning to realize his goal. This does not sit well with Ty, who may have learned how to play nice with others but is never going to satisfy himself. "If it takes me a while, I'll get mad and think about it all night," he says. "I mean, I'm never going to change entirely. I couldn't if I wanted to."

Great activation is the bridge that ensures your public brand aligns with your brand strategy. And it is powerful when it is completely authentic, relevant, and valuable to the target. Good brand activation consistently executes the brand strategy across all aspects of your life so that, over time, your actions support your goals and vision.

BREAKING DOWN THE BRAND ACTIVATION PLAN

A simple way to develop a brand activation plan is to list desired activation activities and then think through if and how well those activities connect to your brand strategy (the Brand Essence Statement from Chapter 6). Your "reasons to believe" are a guide to the choices you should make to activate your brand.

In your brand activation plan, your reasons to believe and other elements from your BES will appear in the left column.

The right column lists the actions you want to take to activate your brand in ways that will strengthen those reasons to believe in your brand. Be honest. If any action steps seem like a stretch to connect to your brand essence, erase it. As you can see in the Ty Jerome example in **Figure 8**, he chose two key action steps to ensure he consistently delivers a superior work ethic. The first action step was centered on putting in outsized effort and practice. The second was working especially hard during the summer when most people take a lot of time off.

Here is Ty Jerome's brand activation plan from his time as a point guard on the UVA men's basketball team.

Figure 8. Ty Jerome's brand activation plan.

Brand Essence Element	Brand Activation Action Steps
Superb Work Ethic Committed to outworking anyone and everyone.	Shows up one hour before practice to work on ball handling/shooting and a half hour after to get up even more shots. In total, commits an average of 7 hours per day to all things basketball, with 2 weeks off in the summer for recovery (practice, weightlifting, conditioning, film, extra workouts).
Outlearn Others Committed to studying and learning about the craft of basketball to enable better performance.	Rewatches entire games and all of practices after playing. Watches film of opponent before every game. Asks offense/defense-related questions during film sessions to improve game plan. Watches 15-minute condensed highlight videos of NBA and other college games everyday.
Team Leader Earns the respect of his teammates through his dedication to helping others perform their best.	Always demonstrates a positive team-first approach in press conferences by praising others. Wins over fans and teammates with grit and dedication to the game of basketball. Models high expectations by outworking everybody. Constructive, real, and honest with others: holds the team to very high expectations.

While creating an activation plan may seem simple, it is actually quite hard. There are three pitfalls brand strategists fall into when developing activation plans:

1. The Plan Is Too Big. A very common mistake is to create a huge activation plan. You have limited hours and resources to invest. The bigger and more complicated the plan is, the lower the likelihood you will be able to implement it effectively.

2. The Action Steps Don't Deliver the Brand. One reason brands don't achieve their potential is that the action steps don't map onto the brand. Consider Jerome's first action step (to get to practice early and stay late), which is intended to support his "superior work ethic" reason to believe from his BES. Let's assume that every basketball player gets to practice 30 minutes early and stays 30 minutes late. Will Jerome's plan deliver a *superior* work ethic? No. It will only deliver a work ethic that is on par with the entire team.

3. The Action Steps Don't Align. When you are developing an activation plan, you want to ensure that the combination of action steps work together to help you accomplish your brand strategy. For example, if Jerome's actions included one bullet point that was focused on beating teammates on some dimension

and another bullet point that emphasized building camaraderie, it is possible that the two action steps could conflict. When you complete the activation plan, step back and make sure that all the actions work well together.

The objective of the activation plan is to align your "brand behavior"—everything you do and say—with your brand strategy. The preceding chapters addressed the importance of setting up guardrails. These guardrails come into play as you develop your activation plan, as they help you develop the boundaries of potential action steps you will and will not take.

EXERCISE NINE
Developing Your Brand
Activation Plan

Using the blank template, complete the following steps. Take your time. This is a critical exercise as it determines whether you will be able to achieve the brand you aspire to have.

1. Brainstorm a list of ideas you can include in your action plan.

2. Analyze your brainstormed list. Which ideas do you think you can achieve? Which ones do you think will be hard to do? Which combination of action steps do you have confidence you can execute? Will they work well together?

3. Write the actions steps in the second column.

4. Think about how each action step connects to your brand essence. Which ideas, if you execute them with excellence, will effectively deliver the reasons to believe in your brand?

5. Write down what part of your brand essence each action step supports and how.

6. Step back and look at the completed activation plan. Pressure test it. Is the plan achievable? Do you believe it will effectively deliver the reasons to believe? Do the action steps fit together coherently or might they send confusing mixed messages about your brand? What worries you about the plan? How might you minimize those worries? Are there any unnecessary or redundant steps that you can eliminate to simplify your plan?

Brand Essence Element	Brand Activation Action Steps

CHAPTER 10

Tweet Intentions

A Case Study on Activating Your Athlete Brand

> " The social media landscape changes incredibly fast, so you have to be open-minded and nimble to keep up with it. "
>
> *—Alexis Ohanian,*
>
> cofounder of Reddit and husband of tennis legend Serena Williams

Just as a casual player who can run up and down a court bouncing a basketball isn't an expert at playing or coaching high-level basketball, few individuals who casually use social media actually understand how to leverage it to create long-term brand value.

Using social media to activate an athlete brand also presents significant risk, as a number of collegiate athletes have found. A series of tweets that then–Wyoming quarterback Josh Allen had posted when he was in high school surfaced shortly before the NFL draft, spurring a media controversy and social media firestorm. "It sucks," Allen told ESPN before the draft. "My family is hurting. We never envisioned a day or night like this." [36] Allen, who was considered a strong candidate to be the no. 1 overall pick and first

quarterback drafted, was ultimately the third quarterback drafted with the seventh overall pick. The difference in income? Quarterback Baker Mayfield, who was selected no. 1 overall by the Cleveland Browns, signed a four-year rookie contract worth $32.7 million with a $21.8 million signing bonus.[37] At no. 7, Allen signed a four-year deal worth $21.1 million with a $13.5 million signing bonuss.[38] That's roughly a $20 million difference. Even the player drafted one spot ahead of Allen at no. 6 signed a deal worth $4 million more. While it is uncertain whether Allen's pre-draft controversy caused him to slide on draft day, how would you feel if your Twitter history might have cost millions of dollars?

Now that you've learned the principles of activating your athlete brand, this chapter provides a case study in activation on one social media platform—Twitter, a popular social media platform for athletes.

Although the following example is based on Twitter, the concepts can be generally exported to any other social media platform. This chapter is designed to detail some simple ways to get started successfully on Twitter for a 20-minute-a-week investment. Look to the Twitter profile of professional dart player Fallon Sherrock.

Why Fallon Sherrock? Because, like the majority of SAs, she plays a sport not considered "mainstream," and her target audience is therefore well-defined and niche, as it should be for many SAs building their brand on Twitter. As the first woman to beat a man at the Professional Darts Corporation World Championship on December 17, 2019, she also offers intriguing insights into how a solid social media presence aligned with a brand can serve as a springboard when an athlete has a moment that catapults them from obscurity to fame overnight.

GETTING STARTED: LEVERAGING TWITTER TO BUILD YOUR ATHLETE BRAND [39]

1. Set an objective. What do you hope to accomplish? Sherrock's big moment came in late 2019, but she joined Twitter in 2010. Scroll through her account, and it's clear it has been dedicated to her brand as a professional dart player for years—whether that means engaging with fellow professional dart players or dart fans, providing updates on events, or tweeting about her sponsors. Because she had set her objective before December 17, 2019, she was able to continue tweeting in the same fashion, preserving her authenticity and credibility (but with many more followers, likes, and engagements).

2. Identify your target. Who is your audience? Luckily, you already figured this out in Chapter 6! Sherrock's target is the darts community, primarily professional darts fans. While this most often means she posts content about her performances and events, she also shares content on behalf of her sponsors to help them reach her fans. As an athlete, your target audience will "consume" your social media content. How you engage with people via social media will impact what they think of your brand and can influence their decision-making about you. While you most likely will want to use social media to target fans of the teams you play on, you will always need to stay focused on doing this in a way that also helps you achieve your goals. That often

means considering what coaches, scouts, teammates, and recruiters might think of your posts.

3. Create a strong Twitter handle. Just as naming a product matters, your Twitter handle (i.e., your Twitter name) matters. Shorter handles make it easier for others to tweet, because of the limitation on characters. Odd spellings, odd names, and common handles make it difficult to remember or find you on Twitter. You want your handle to be simple, memorable, and linked to who you are. Though there are risks, SAs should generally focus on using their name in some form as it is easier for your target to remember. Sherrock chose @Fsherrock. Sherrock isn't a common name, so it's easy to find her on Twitter.

4. Create a strong bio: Your bio is quite important because it is the essence of your brand. Who are you? You want this to be relevant to your target because many people decide to follow or not follow you based solely on your bio. Just as the headline of a print ad often determines whether somebody will read any additional copy, your bio determines whether people find you interesting and relevant enough to follow.

• How do you design a strong bio? It should start with the

information that matters to your target. Sherrock likes to dance, but it's not in her profile because it's not important or relevant to her target. Here is Sherrock's current Twitter bio:

"Professional Dart Player & Queen of the Palace. Enq events@modussports.com @ModusDarts180 @Servicesure @LstyleEurope @DYNASTY_JAPAN @FinanceCastle #usedSOFT"

• Note that Sherrock included the primary topic (Professional Dart Player). Of note, the hashtag (#) is one method by which individuals can search for relevant topics on Twitter.

• Figure 9 provides a few examples of different types of athlete bios on Twitter. Sherrock's bio fits the mold of one highlighting sponsors.[40]

5. Tweet on topics relevant to your target. This is where consistency and discipline come in. If you tweet about cooking, marketing, Australia, golf, puppies, and college, it will be challenging to develop a clear brand and difficult for any fan to know why they should follow you. Your brand should be easily discernible to anybody viewing your posts. Sherrock tweets almost exclusively about content

Figure 9. Example Twitter profiles.

BIO HIGHLIGHTING ACCOLADES

NAME: Elena Delle Donne

SPORT: Basketball

TWITTER HANDLE: @De11eDonne

BIO: 2015 and 2019 WNBA MVP | 50-40-90 Club | 2013 WNBA Rookie of the Year | Washington Mystics #11 Delaware Native!

BUSINESS INQUIRES CONTACT: @ErinKane

BIO HIGHLIGHTING PERSONAL INFORMATION

NAME: Michael Phelps

SPORT: Swimming

TWITTER HANDLE: @MichaelPhelps

BIO: Husband to @MrsNicolePhelps | Dad to Boomer, Beckett, Maverick | Pet Dad to Juno & Legend | Water Safety & Mental Health Advocate | Gold Medalist

BIO HIGHLIGHTING PASSION

NAME: Serena Williams

SPORT: Tennis

TWITTER HANDLE: @serenawilliams

BIO: Living, Loving, and working to help you.

BIO HIGHLIGHTING MOTIVATION

NAME: Odell Beckham Jr.

SPORT: Football

TWITTER HANDLE: @obj

BIO: The toughest part of getting to the top of the ladder, is getting through the crowd at the bottom. #UndeniableTruth #DestinedForGreatness #GodSpeed #YM

BIO HIGHLIGHTING AFFILIATIONS & SPONSORS

NAME: RJ Barrett

SPORT: Basketball

TWITTER HANDLE: @RjBarrett6

BIO: Team Canada | Class of 2018 | UPlay | Montverde Academy | Duke | New York Knicks | PUMA

BIO HIGHLIGHTING BELIEFS

NAME: Clayton Kershaw

SPORT: Baseball

TWITTER HANDLE: @ClaytonKersh22

BIO: Colossians 3:23

related to professional darts. Every now and then, she will tweet about something outside of this focus, but more than 90% of her tweets and retweets are centered on achieving her objective: being an influencer of and engaging with darts fans.

- Importantly, this clarity of content strategy is the shift that needs to happen when you migrate from using social media as a consumer (to connect with friends) to leverage it to build your athlete brand. Sherrock doesn't use Twitter for personal, intimate friendships. It's public.

- SAs should be aware that more companies, coaches, and agents are now conducting background searches on prospective employees' social media habits. In 2016, a then–wide receivers coach for the Arkansas Razorbacks tweeted, "Came across an awful Twitter account today. Shame, the kid was a really good player...On to the next one...get a clue!"[41] Remember the lesson from Chapter 8: you are in a symbiotic relationship. As you move beyond college and strive to work for a professional team or enter another profession, those organizations will be checking to see if your brand fits theirs. One recommendation to help think through this is to connect with

your school media or marketing organization to ensure that what you are tweeting and posting will positively build your brand.

6. **Minimize the risk:** You want to create discipline by constructing guardrails that guide all content to ensure you minimize the downside. Make sure to use the guardrails you constructed in Chapter 7 and check with your school's media or marketing groups to minimize risk. It is very important to always be conscious of what you are portraying and signaling through your profile.

7. **Start tweeting...slowly:** An easy way to start is to identify 10 people who are influential in your content area and then simply retweet their tweets. For Sherrock's content area, she could have Googled "world's best dart players" or "professional darts sponsors" when she first sought to grow her brand as a dart player. She'd identify 10 individuals or brands and then look them up, follow them, and retweet them. Benefits of starting this way include the following:

- You limit your risk because you are retweeting a best-in-class influencer in the space.

- It's fast (it only takes a minute to look up somebody influential and retweet their post).

- You are building your network with high-quality people (most leaders in social media will follow you back if you follow them).

- It's smart to "apprentice" by observing the habits of leading influencers while you're in learning mode (but be careful not to create a large disparity in the number you follow versus followers as it may signal that you are desperate for followers).

Remember to tweet original content in addition to retweets. A general rule that businesses keep in mind is the 80/20 rule: 80% of your posts should "inform, educate, and entertain," while 20% should promote your brand.[42]

The internet is full of tips and resources to help you grow your followers on Twitter and other social media channels. Once you've followed these steps to start using Twitter as part of a brand strategy, experiment with those tips to grow your following. Just be sure that those tips and strategies align with your brand strategy.

FROM TWITTER TO TOMORROW: HOW TO BE STRATEGIC ACROSS SOCIAL MEDIA

As you can see, just activating a brand via Twitter can be challenging. If you want to build your brand via social media, you have to develop the content and post it across different platforms, such as TikTok, Instagram, and so forth. This takes time, and every new platform, post, and image carries risk. However, building a social media presence will help you activate your brand and achieve certain goals if you are disciplined and strategic about it. It can benefit you, but it takes months and years to develop a following and build a brand. With the new NIL landscape, the opportunities that can be created from an athlete brand engaging on social media are numerous.

EXERCISE TEN
Shift from Being a Consumer of Social Media to a Strategist

As you've seen, strategists approach social media differently than do consumers. Take a minute to think about who you follow on social media, assess who among those you follow is a compelling "model" with regards to social media posts, and write down lessons you observe and want to employ. Then evaluate your own social media bio and posts (if you have social media accounts).

1. Who are the top athletes you follow?

How would you assess their effectiveness at building a clear, consistent, and effective (for the long term) brand? Why?

2. Why are some athlete bios/posts more effective than others? What lessons have you observed that you want to remember?

3. Assess your social media accounts. How would you improve the bios and posts?

CHAPTER

11

More Money,
More Problems

What You Need to Know
Before You Monetize Your Brand

> **An athlete cannot run with money in his pockets. He must run with hope in his heart and dreams in his head.**
>
> *—Emil Zátopek,*
>
> ranked the Greatest Runner of All Time by *Runner's World*, the only runner in history to win gold in the 5,000-meter, 10,000-meter, and marathon races in a single Olympic Games

With your brand designed and a clear sense of how to activate your brand strategy, it's time to shift gears to think about how to monetize your brand. Remember when you started this book? You were probably thinking, "Let's start monetizing!" even before you opened it. Now you know there should be a lot of intentional work and planning before you start monetizing your athlete brand in a way that actually serves your goals.

If you've read carefully and completed every exercise to this point, you are technically prepared to start making monetization decisions. However, there are still a few things you should know first before jumping in.

1. Brand activation and monetization requires effort. It doesn't happen on its own. You have to invest your resources: time and, in some cases, money. If you decide that you want to grow your social media presence, it can take hours a week, over the course of years, to develop a strong following. For some, it can happen faster. But there is no guarantee. If you want to sign autographs, then you have to invest time going to places where your fans congregate and signing objects until your hand goes numb. You will need to decide how much you want to invest, and then reallocate your resources accordingly.

2. In the long run, there will be infinite ways to monetize an athlete brand, and they do not all deliver the same value. Monetization opportunities will not all deliver equal benefits

or create equal risk. If you sign autographs, there is almost no risk (assuming you don't talk much). In contrast, social media is never-ending risk. One post or comment can damage a brand. On the flip side, signing an autograph does not deliver ongoing value, while a strong social media following does. You make money once off an autograph. To make money again, you need to sign another autograph. However, if you have 50,000 social media followers, they likely will stay with you, enabling you to make money off the value of your fans year after year (i.e., an "annuity" benefit).

In addition to each method delivering different value, each also can require different resources. For example, signing autographs might take 30 minutes after home games. Social media may take two to three hours per week. There is a concept in finance called return on investment, or ROI. How much money are you able to make given a certain amount of resource (e.g., time) investment?

Table 2 is a grid that highlights how common monetization options (e.g., camps, modeling, personal work product, etc.) can be evaluated across seven different dimensions. The seven dimensions are as follows:

1. Level of brand risk: how much personal risk is associated with the activity
2. Time commitment: how much time is required to invest in the activity
3. Potential to build long-term brand value (versus a short-term monetary benefit)
4. Ability to control whether you engage in the channel (i.e., you are not dependent on somebody else wanting to hire you)
5. Guaranteed return: degree to which you are guaranteed income based on your effort
6. Fit with your brand strategy
7. Potential for you to make money

The last two dimensions are specific to each SA. Some SAs will make more via social media than others. Others, however, may make more signing autographs or modeling. You need to assess each of these methods given your brand strategy, your goals, and how much money you need to make or want to make given the effort required.

As you evaluate the grid, you will notice that the different monetization channels have varying strengths and weaknesses across the first five evaluation dimensions. Some channels require more time. Others provide you with greater control. Still others have higher levels of risk. You'll also note that some might vary depending on the engagement. For example, the time commitment associated with "promotional appearances" varies depending on the nature of the engagement. Somebody could hire you to show up for a one-hour event. Somebody else might want you to show up for a weekly event.

This grid is designed to be a starting point for you to think about which channels might work best to help you attain your goals. You might want to add your own rows to it. Further, you will want to evaluate any specific opportunities using these different dimensions. Unfortunately, there is no way to see the monetization options of the future. But this framework can be a useful way to consider alternative options.

Table 2. Brand monetization option assessment grid.

	Risk Level	Time Commitment	Long-Term Brand Building Effect	Barrier to Entry	Investment Assurance	Fit with Your Brand Strategy	Potential for You to Make Money
Camps, Clinics, Lessons	Medium	Depends	Potential to be Strong	Medium	High		
Personal Work Product— Excluding Social Media	Medium	Depends	Medium	Medium	High		
Personal Work Product— Social Media	High	Significant over Time	Potential to be Strong	Low	Low		
Sales of Memorabilia, Equipment, etc.	Low	Nominal	Low	Medium	Mesium		
Autographs	Low	Nominal	Low	Medium	Potential to be High		
Promotional Appearances	Medium	Depends	Potential to be Strong	High	High (assuming contract)		
Modeling	Low	Nominal	Potential to be Strong	High	High (assuming contract)		
Brand Ambassador	Mediom	Depends	Medium	Medium	High (assuming contract)		
Speaking Engagements and Appearances	Medium	Depends	Potential to be Strong	High	High (assuming contract)		

3. Be strategic about which channels of monetization you pick, at what time, and why. Each monetization channel requires a different level of your time and effort and delivers different value (e.g., money, brand-building exposure, etc.). This will vary for every athlete. Some will enter college with a significant social media presence. Some will enter with a very desirable public image that companies will want to associate with, and therefore hire them to be a spokesperson. There is no one-size-fits-all approach. This requires you to think about your assets, how much you want out of your monetization efforts, and how much you are willing to invest to achieve your monetization goals.

A POINT ABOUT THE PROMISE AND PERILS OF BRAND MONETIZATION

Whether it is $2,000, $200,000, or even more, the idea of making money from your name, image, and likeness is enticing. But the question is: "At what cost?" Your time is valuable—it is your most precious resource. You can invest your time in building your brand for the future by strengthening your athletic performance, preparing for a post-college athletic career, or improving your academic performance. Or you can invest your time in leveraging your current brand to make money. It is hard to focus on everything, and the allure of short-term money can potentially get in the way of long-term money.

As an example of how this works, consider Ty Jerome (and his brand activation plan in Chapter 9). UVA Coach Tony Bennett called him the Tom Brady of the 2019 NCAA championship UVA basketball team. While Jerome was in college, it was evident that he was nearly completely focused on his sport (just look at his activation plan!). He had a vision to make it to the NBA and nothing was going to get in the way of accomplishing this goal. As described earlier, after suffering the most embarrassing of losses in the 2018 NCAA tournament, he spent the next summer living in the gym. Can you imagine that Jerome would have spent much time focused on monetizing his brand (if it had been available to him in 2018)? Would he have let that impact his investment in building his athletic capability?

To make this point more vivid, fast forward and look at Jerome now as an NBA player. In a discussion about his goals as an NBA player, he said he is focused *only on basketball*. In fact, as he transitioned into the NBA, he interviewed six or seven prospective agents and sidestepped those who wanted to focus on sponsorships, marketing, and non-basketball opportunities. He chose his current agent because the agent understood Jerome. His mission is to become the very best basketball player possible, playing for several years (OK, Jerome said "15 years") in the NBA. Everything else is a distraction.

Think about how this works from a financial perspective. If Jerome earns three contracts in the NBA, he will have made a lot of money purely from basketball. Drafted no. 24 in the NBA in 2018, he is on track to make more than $6 million over the final season of his contract. When it is time to sign a second contract in 2023, Jerome's performance will dictate the value, but his minimum annual salary will be more than $2 million per year, and the average NBA salary is nearly $8 million per year. If he is still playing basketball in 10 years, how much will he have made?

Now go back and imagine the time he might have taken during college trying to make $20,000 or $200,000. Was his laser focus on his sport the "right" investment of his time? Remember, Jerome was not a sure-fire NBA draft pick. He was knocked for his lack of athleticism, which he makes up for through working harder and learning more than competitors.

There is a saying that you don't ever want to step over a dollar to pick up a nickel. In this case, Jerome would have understood that forgoing short-term small money to invest in a successful pro career was far more lucrative—and smarter.

However, each SA's conditions differ and so the importance of short-term money varies. You need to pick the right approach given your specific circumstances.

EXERCISE ELEVEN
Key Questions to Answer Before Monetization

Brand activation doesn't necessarily require you to reallocate your time because activation activities can simply be how you show up for class, practice, games, and post-game interviews. However, brand monetization is definitely an additional activity that will require you to reallocate time.

To help you think through your monetization options, answer each of the following questions and then complete your time allocation chart again, this time adding in time for brand monetization. Your answers to the five questions should help you start to identify the types of monetization activities you will want to prioritize and how much time they will take.

1. What are your assets? Do you have a strong social media presence? Are you very photogenic (unfair as it may be, personal appearance— and how that appearance matches a company brand— drives many company marketing and advertising decisions)? Do you have connections and resources in specific areas?

2. Review your goals. Which monetization channels fit best with your goals? If you want to reach the Olympics, how does brand monetization fit with your goals and aspirations?

3. What strengths and resources does your school have regarding each of the monetization channels? Some schools and teams may have developed capabilities in some of the monetization channels, such as a regular method for providing autographs or a unique partnership with an athletic apparel brand. This would require less time on your part because the school is creating the opportunity.

4. How much time are you willing to invest? In Chapter 4, you allocated your time across the different categories. How much time per week do you want to invest in monetization, and where will the time come from?

5. After considering your assets, goals, the school's resources, and your time allocation, which monetization channels fit best? This should be where you prioritize your efforts.

Now that you have decided how monetization will fit into your life and help you achieve your goals, revise your time allocation chart to incorporate your investment in brand monetization.

SLEEP

Hours

Priority Activities

ACADEMIC

Hours

Priority Activities

ATHLETIC

Hours

Priority Activities

PERSONAL

Hours

Priority Activities

ACTIVATION

Hours

Priority Activities

REBECCA JARRETT'S ANSWERS TO THE PRELIMINARY MONETIZATION QUESTIONS

1. What are your assets? Do you have a strong social media presence? Are you very photogenic? Do you have connections and resources in specific areas?

> My current social media presence is fairly weak as I have not prioritized it. I have been told that I am photogenic and I enjoy taking photos.

2. Review your goals. Which monetization channels fit best with your goals? If you want to reach the Olympics, how does brand monetization fit with your goals and aspirations?

> I don't want to invest more than two hours a week developing a path to monetization. My priorities are: 1) social media, 2) business development/ personal work product, and 3) personal appearances/ autographs. The first two priorities fit well with my short-term soccer interest as well as my long-term business interest.

3. What strengths and resources does your school have regarding each of the monetization channels?

> Given the recent decision on NIL, it is unclear what resources the school will be providing. However, I don't have many additional connections or access to resources (specifically related to my top 3 monetization channels listed above) outside of those afforded to me through Virginia Athletics.

Note: This might be a common response for those at the start of their brand journey. However, most schools—especially in the quickly emerging NIL era—have resources to support you. Ask your coaches and the member of the athletics department assigned to support your sport.

4. How much time are you willing to invest? How much time per week do you want to invest in monetization, and where will the time come from?

> Not more than two hours per week.

5. After considering your assets, goals, the school's resources, and your time allocation, which monetization channels fit best? This should be where you prioritize your efforts.

> My priorities are: 1) social media, 2) business development/personal work product, and 3) personal appearances/autographs.

CHAPTER 12

Excuse Me, Can I Have
Your Autograph?

Monetizing Your Brand

> " Building a profitable personal brand is not just about followers and channels. Rather, it is related to the ability to convert brand authority into profit. "
>
> —*Dr. Talaya Waller,*
>
> author of *The Monetization of Personal Brands*, entrepreneur, and public speaker, including the TEDx Talk "The Future of Branding Is Personal"

At this point, you have started thinking about the different ways you can monetize your brand and, more importantly, begun to think strategically about how you want to allocate your resources (i.e., time) to help you achieve all your goals—not just your short-term financial goals.

The challenge with brand monetization is that, if you are not careful, you can start investing a lot of time in activities that will increase short-term income at the cost of long-term goal attainment.

And don't forget the reputational risks, as discussed in Chapter 10 with the case of quarterback Josh Allen's tweet controversy before the NFL draft. In a world where what you do and say at the age of 14 can follow you for years, the need to ensure that you protect your brand—by doing and saying things that will be beneficial in 10, 20, and 40 years—is more important than ever. All of this means that young athletes need to operate with a great deal more responsibility than an average 18-year-old does. That's why this book is designed to help you approach these decisions in a strategic manner, rather than an opportunistic or short-sighted manner.

HOW TO PICK YOUR MONETIZATION CHANNELS AND DEVELOP A PLAN

There are three steps to develop a monetization plan that allows you to pursue income opportunities that best align with your brand and goals.

1. Begin by identifying the monetization activities in which you want to invest. As NIL policies evolve, the ways in which you can monetize your brand will change. Find out from your school what monetization options are available to you. Then identify which options you want to pursue and how much time per week you want to invest (and where that time will come from).

   For example, assume that Mamadi, a water polo player, has decided he wants to invest 30 minutes per week into monetization and wants to focus on activities that minimize risks. Assume Mamadi doesn't believe that he has any easy access to modeling opportunities and that camps are not a big money-maker for water polo players. He believes his best option, to minimize time and risk while maximizing alignment with his brand and short-term income, will be to take advantage of his school's efforts to sell autographs. See an example in **Table 3a** of how Mamadi would fill out the grid.

2. Second, it is time to develop a monetization plan. Recall how you developed your brand activation plan in Chapter 9? You will do something similar to develop your monetization plan. In the fifth column in the table in **Exercise 12**, you will identify the "action steps" you plan to take to monetize your brand.

   Look at the completed Mamadi example in **Table 3b**. In this case, Mamadi has decided to leverage the school's autograph efforts. Consequently, his action steps include talking with his coaches about his plan, working with the athletic department to identify dates and times for autograph sessions, coordinating his academic and social schedules to ensure there are no time conflicts, and so forth.

3. Once you have developed your monetization plan, you should add it to your brand activation plan from Chapter 9. Monetization is really just another aspect of your brand activation plan, but it is broken out separately in this book because 1) monetization through NIL is "what's new" in the world of college athlete branding and 2) monetization tends to steal effort and attention when your focus should be on the fundamentals of brand activation efforts that advance goal attainment.

Table 3a. Mamadi's monetization planning grid.

Monetization Options*	Invest In? (Yes/No)	How Much Time per Week?	Activity Comes from What Investment?
Camps, Clinics, Lessons	No		
Business Development/ Personal Work Product	No		
Sales of Memorabilia, Apparel, and Equipment	No		
Autographs	Yes	30 min.	Sleep
Promotional Appearances and Activities	No		
Modeling	No		
Brand Ambassador	No		
Speaking Engagements and Personal Appearances	No		
Musician, Artist, Author	No		
Professional Services: Agents, Lawyers, and Money Managers	No		

Update this list based on your state's laws and NCAA rulings.

Notice the hypothetical example from Ty Jerome in **Figure 10**. Now his plan includes a fourth brand element that is focused on monetization. Your plan must be appropriate for you, based on the time you have, the sport you play, and your goals. There is no "one-size-fits-all."

Table 3b. Mamadi's completed monetization plan.

Monetization Options*	Invest In? (Yes/No)	How Much Time per Week?	Activity Comes from What Investment?	Monetization Plan
Camps, Clinics, Lessons	No			
Business Development/ Personal Work Product	No			
Sales of Memorabilia, Apparel, and Equipment	No			
Autographs	Yes	30 min.	Sleep	1. Talk to coaches for support and counsel (July) 2. Talk to Athletic Dept. to identify process (August) 3. Sign up for autograph sessions
Promotional Appearances and Activities	No			
Modeling	No			
Brand Ambassador	No			
Speaking Engagements and Personal Appearances	No			
Musician, Artist, Author	No			
Professional Services: Agents, Lawyers, and Money Managers	No			

*Update this list based on your state's laws and NCAA rulings.

Figure 10. Ty Jerome's brand activation plan including monetization.

Brand Essence Element	Brand Activation Action Steps
Superb Work Ethic Committed to outworking anyone and everyone.	Shows up one hour before practice to work on ball handling/shooting and a half hour after to get up even more shots. In total, commits an average of 7 hours per day to all things basketball, with 2 weeks off in the summer for recovery (practice, weightlifting, conditioning, film, extra workouts).
Outlearn Others Committed to studying and learning about the craft of basketball to enable better performance.	Rewatches entire games and all of practices after playing. Watches film of opponent before every game. Asks offense/defense-related questions during fil sessions to improve game plan. Watches 15-minute condensed highlight videos of NBA and other college games everyday.
Team Leader Earns the respect of his teammates through his dedication to helping others perform their best.	Always demonstrates a positive team-first approach in press conferences by praising others. Wins over fans and teammates with grit and dedication to the game of basketball. Models high expectations by outworking everybody. Constructive, real, and honest with others: holds the team to very high expectations.
Monetize Brand Emphasize long-term brand development while meeting financial short-term goals ($15k/year)	Invest in long-term building brand via social media—minimize risk by only talking about basketball in a positive way (30 min./week). Leverage UVA marketing team to augment social media efforts and use UVA assets (photos, videos, etc.). Finance short-term needs via autographs (30 min./week).

EXERCISE
TWELVE
Develop Your
Monetization Plan

It's now your turn to follow the three steps detailed above to create your monetization plan.

1. In the first three columns of the table, identify which options you want to pursue and how much time you want to invest per week (and

where that time will come from). This book provides a list of common monetization activities, but you will need to update the options based on updates from the NCAA and the state where your university is located. Your school athletics department will have information on types of monetization that comply with the rules.

Monetization Options*	Invest In? (Yes/No)	How Much Time per Week?	Activity Comes from What Investment?	Monetization Plan
Camps, Clinics, Lessons				
Business Development/ Personal Work Product				
Sales of Memorabilia, Apparel, and Equipment				
Autographs				
Promotional Appearances and Activities				

Monetization Options*	Invest In? (Yes/No)	How Much Time per Week?	Activity Comes from What Investment?	Monetization Plan
Modeling				
Brand Ambassador				
Speaking Engagements and Personal Appearances				
Musician, Artist, Author				
Professional Services: Agents, Lawyers, and Money Managers				

2. In the final column, identify the action steps you plan to take to monetize your brand.

3. Finish up your brand activation plan by adding your monetization plan to it (as seen in **Figure 10**, the example of Ty Jerome's activation plan).

Brand Essence Element	Brand Activation Action Steps
Monetize Brand Emphasize long-term brand development while meeting financial short-term goals ($15k/year)	

CHAPTER 13

Athlete, Chief Branding Officer . . . and Data Scientist?

Assessing and Measuring Your Brand

> ❝ **When you cannot measure it, when you cannot express it in numbers, your knowledge is of a meager and unsatisfactory kind.** ❞
>
> *—William Thompson,*
>
> better known as Lord Kelvin, 19th-century British physicist, inventor, and investor famous for refining the accuracy of units of measurement for electricity and energy

You have developed your brand strategy and created an activation plan, including a monetization plan. You know how important it is to be strategic in building your brand to accomplish both your short- and long-term goals. You understand the upside—and downside—of trying to monetize your brand. The last thing that is important to understand is that brands are dynamic. They change. Veteran athletes like Lindsey Vonn, Lionel Messi, Tom Brady, and Serena Williams do not have the same brand strategy that they would have had at age 18. Over time, their goals change. The ways in which they want to make an impact change. And with higher incomes, the amount of risk they may be willing to take changes as well.

Consequently, it is important for you to go through the exercises in this book at least once per year to assess: update your goals, brand strategy, and activation plan (including the monetization aspects) as needed. Has anything changed? If so, how does that impact your brand strategy and your activation plan? The beauty of going through these exercises regularly is that, at some point, you will begin to naturally update your brand strategy and plan. You will become more adept at managing and building your brand—whether you stay in sports or pursue some other career. The process you use here doesn't change whether you are an athlete or a coach or an engineer.

In addition to assessing your brand, you will need to set up some ways to regularly measure how your brand is performing against your strategy and plan. Simple and useful metrics for SAs might include the following:

- Social media followers and engagements (e.g., likes, comments, etc.)

- New branding leads (e.g., people reaching out to request you as a spokesperson or to appear at an event, endorsement offers, interview requests, etc.)

- Mentions in traditional and social media

- Page views of owned content (e.g., YouTube videos or blog posts)

- Time spent and income received from monetization channels

You should regularly (weekly or monthly) review your activation plan and look at your metrics. What do your metrics tell you about your efforts? Are your metrics meeting or beating the plan? Should they be adjusted? Also, make fast friends with your athletic department's marketing group. They can provide some of the data on the above metrics.

TIPS FOR MEASURING AND UPDATING YOUR BRAND, ACTIVATION, AND MONETIZATION PLANS

1. Go through all the exercises in this book annually. Select a day each year and put it on your calendar. Pick a day when you will have time and be motivated to reflect and consider the future. New Year's Day, for instance, is a natural time to reflect on the past year and to begin planning for the next.

2. Update all the metrics you track either weekly or monthly. Schedule this on your calendar as a "to-do" action item. It should only take about 10 minutes, but it is important to get in the habit of measuring your progress against your plan. Plans are only as good as your ability to deliver them. As the quote at the beginning of the chapter suggests, measuring progress is a key to ensuring you deliver.

CHAPTER 14

The End Is the Beginning

Continuing Your Brand Journey

> ❝ I can accept failure, everyone fails at something. But I can't accept not trying. ❞
>
> —*Michael Jordan,*
>
> NBA Hall of Fame basketball player, six-time NBA champion, majority owner of the Charlotte Hornets, and partner in Nike's Jordan brand

What better athlete to conclude this book than Michael Jordan—the basketball legend *Sports Illustrated* argues has the strongest athlete brand of all time and "opened every marketing dollar in the world for every future athlete"?

The point of highlighting Michael Jordan's words to start this final chapter is twofold. First, while every SA might want to "Be Like Mike" in terms of athletic and brand performance, few will ever rival his success in either measure.

But that's OK. And that leads to the second point, which is what Jordan is actually saying. Life is about trying, effort, experimentation, and—yes—failure. All these lead to improvement. If you are reading this, you are likely soon to be a college SA, are an SA,

or were an SA. So you already know this is true. You discovered a game and started to get better through practice and play. At a certain point, as you improved and became more serious about your sport, you probably started watching more tape, spending more time in the gym, setting goals, making detailed improvement plans, and investing in resources to grow your skills.

Along the way, you experienced success and failure. Perhaps you even reached a ceiling in your athletic performance that fell short of your goals. But you never know what your ceiling really is if you don't try.

That process—and Jordan's quote— apply word-for-word to your efforts to develop, activate, and monetize your athlete brand. And in that sense, the end of this book is only the beginning of your work and your journey to build a strong brand and capitalize on your name, image, and likeness.

FINISHING WHERE WE STARTED

By trusting the process laid out in this book and working step by step through the exercises, you have gained the skills to do four things:

1. Identify your vision, goals, and resources

2. Define your brand

3. Activate your brand

4. Monetize your brand

Congratulations! By getting to this point, you have taken a crash course in Branding 101. You've learned some of the fundamentals and skills that marketers have been using to propel multibillion-dollar brands for decades, and they are just as relevant to your athlete brand as they are to brands like Nike or Gatorade.

Take a look at **Figure 11**. Do you remember this graphic from Chapter 1? It might not have made perfect sense then, but likely it does now. Your brand should be built after understanding

Figure 11. The branding process.

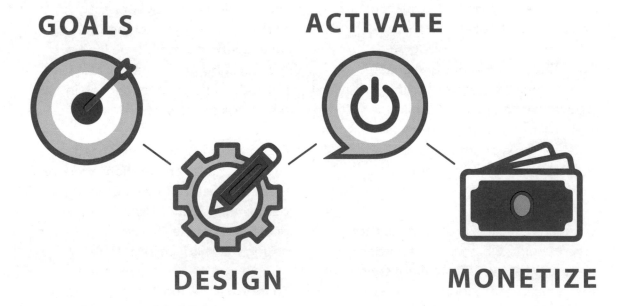

GOALS

ACTIVATE

DESIGN

MONETIZE

your goals and resources. As you develop and activate your brand, it should create new opportunities to redefine your goals and grow your resources. Your brand is a continuous journey, and it's one that will require you to keep growing, learning, and adapting.

IF YOU REMEMBER ONE THING, REMEMBER THIS

This book exists because of the groundbreaking decision to allow college athletes to benefit from their name, image, and likeness. The opportunities for you to establish your athlete brands, advance your goals, and earn income while you're at it is astounding. But the opportunity does not come without risks—to your time, energy, and success in sport and life—if you're not careful.

The life of an athlete brand in the public light is not for the faint of heart in this fast-moving, hyper-transparent, overly noisy, ultra-reactionary landscape of the 21st century. But the risk is worth the reward. IF you remember one thing.

Remember what's most important to YOU! Remember what you wrote in the first chapter about why you started this book.

This book is about your goals: the goals you want to accomplish in

your sport and through your sport. Your athlete brand serves those goals. It is not a thing to get rich from or influence others. Those are byproducts of your success in achieving your goals and how well your brand is aligned with those goals.

As you build and refine your athlete brand, don't forget the big picture. Keep your eyes on the prize. It's easy to get off course amid all the noise and distraction. And it will be easy to get excited about the opportunity to monetize your brand. Do you think that if Michael Jordan spent an extra two hours a week monetizing his collegiate brand instead of practicing his sport, he would have been better off? Remember what your brand is supposed to serve, and you'll stay on track.

WHAT'S NEXT?

Hopefully, you've already started to put many of the lessons from this book into practice in the real world. At a minimum, if you've completed the exercises, you have a brand essence statement, brand activation plan, and monetization assessment that you can directly apply in a very practical way to your branding efforts moving forward.

But, to stick with a sports metaphor, you've only just learned to play the game.

Do you remember playing your sport with other beginners? Some probably had a natural talent and picked it up right away. Others were probably terrible and had no natural talent for the game. But you surely know at least a few less-talented athletes who became better than the more naturally talented ones through hard work, practice, and dedication.

You might have a natural talent and instinct for managing your brand in alignment with your goals. Or everything about branding might sound like ancient Greek. Either way, you have room to improve the ways in which you activate your brand. Those who keep working at it diligently, following their plan, will ultimately get the most value from their brand.

As you move forward with your career, do three things next:

1. Get out there. Start practicing. Start experimenting. Manage your time and resources carefully. If you're trying something and it's taking up too much of your time and resources or not advancing your goals, revise your activation plan. When you feel things are drifting the wrong way, check back with your brand essence statement and make sure all your actions and activities flow directly from it.

2. Don't stop learning. This book is a primer to get you started and make sure you have the basic skills and knowledge to have agency managing your brand. But there's so much more to learn in books, online, and elsewhere. As an SA, you also have coaches, professors, and an athletics department staff who want to help you succeed. Not only do they care about you personally, but the success of your athlete brand directly advances their goals, as well. Your interests are aligned. Use your resources and don't be afraid to ask!

3. Keep this book—and your completed exercises—handy. No one reads a book and remembers every lesson and insight. Whether you read this book and completed the exercises straight through or skimmed around, you will need to keep coming back to these core lessons to reinforce and refine your understanding of key concepts. That's the beauty of the structure of this book and its exercises: If you're struggling with your brand in one area, return to the relevant chapter and your completed exercise. Reread the lesson. Revisit your output. Revise your approach. Then go back to no. 1 in this list. As the saying goes, you've drunk from the fire hose. Now be sure to keep taking sips from the water fountain.

Acknowledgements

With Gratitude

We would like to thank the many students, SAs, and members of the University of Virginia Athletics Department staff and UVA community who encouraged us to pursue this project, and whose insider knowledge of the SA experience was essential.

To the UVA Athletics Department and Athletics Director Carla Williams, we are deeply grateful for your endorsement and support and are thankful for the opportunity to advance knowledge and improve the lives of SAs throughout all of college athletics.

To Ted White, former UVA Deputy Athletics Director, this book would not have been possible without your relentless passion and persistence to help SAs learn how to build their athlete brands in a better way—one which aligns with their long-term goals and dreams. You inspired us in so many ways, and we are so very grateful for your essential ongoing input, advice, and counsel to make this book as valuable as possible.

Ty Jerome and Kyle Guy, former UVA men's basketball players turned pro, it has been an honor and pleasure to have your brand stories included in this book. Your commitment and selflessness in helping future generations of SAs speaks volumes about why you have developed such impressive "athlete brands" that garner devoted fans.

Grant Kersey, thank you for being a most valued contributor, providing perspective and counsel throughout the entire process, helping us see this book as other SAs will see it, and your ideas on how to activate the book's potential. It has been a joy to work with you on this (and frankly, to talk about UVA basketball at length)!

Rebecca Jarrett and Liam Nolan, thank you for your creativity, many hours of research, service as "test subjects," and your tireless enthusiasm.

Thomas Rogers and Mamadi Diane, your effort to connect us with the athletics department was the spark that began this journey. You have proven once again that UVA and Darden students are talented leaders, and we know you have great futures ahead.

John Barnett, thank you for your beautiful cover and skilled design. You have woven together a complex tapestry of text, graphics, and exercises in a way that will make learning about branding easier and more enjoyable for SAs.

To the team at Darden Business Publishing, we offer our heartfelt gratitude for the countless hours and attention spent editing and producing this book. Your support went above and beyond. We appreciate both your partnership and understanding that a book to help young athletes and colleges navigate NIL aligned with your mission to advance business knowledge.

And last but certainly not least, to our families and friends. Kim thanks her parents, Robert and Carol Ann Whitler, for their endless support and enthusiasm to help young people unlock the power of marketing. Jay would like to thank his biggest fan, his mother Milly, for her constant encouragement to pursue his passion for writing.

Notes

1. Josh Planos, "How Much Money Could Student-Athletes Make as Social Media Influencers?," *FiveThirtyEight*, May 15, 2020, https://fivethirtyeight.com/features/how-much-money-could-student-athletes-make-as-social-media-influencers/ (accessed Aug. 16, 2021).

2. Stewart Mandel and Nicole Auerbach, "What Could College Athletes' Social Media Brands Be Worth?," *Athletic*, May 7, 2020, https://theathletic.com/1796999/2020/05/07/college-athlete-name-image-likeness-value/ (accessed Aug. 16, 2021).

3. "Board of Governors Moves toward Allowing Student-Athlete Compensation for Endorsements and Promotions," *NCAA*, April 29, 2020, https://www.ncaa.org/about/resources/media-center/news/board-governors-moves-toward-allowing-student-athlete-compensation-endorsements-and-promotions (accessed Aug. 16, 2021).

4. "Our Mission," Brogdon Family Foundation, 2021, https://www.brogdonfamilyfoundation.org/ (accessed Aug. 16, 2021).

5. Lauren Ohnesorge, "Judge Sides with Former Duke Phenom Zion Williamson in Lawsuit against Marketing Agency," *Triangle Business Journal*, January 20, 2021, https://www.bizjournals.com/triangle/news/2021/01/20/judge-ruling-zion-williamson-lawsuit-prime-sports.html (accessed Aug. 16, 2021).

6. John Berman, "Is LeBron James Worth $90 Million?," *ABC News*, January 7, 2006, https://abcnews.go.com/WNT/story?id=129682&page=1 (accessed Aug. 16, 2021).

7. Emmett Knowlton, "LeBron James' Business Partner Confirms Lifetime Deal with Nike Is Worth Over $1 Billion," *Insider*, May 17, 2016, https://www.businessinsider.com/lebron-james-nike-deal-exceeds-1-billion-maverick-carter-says-2016-5 (accessed Aug. 16, 2021).

8. Bennett Conlin, "A Major in Coaching: Walk-on Chase Coleman Pursues Coaching Dreams on UVa's Sideline," *Daily Progress*, January 14, 2021, https://dailyprogress.com/sports/a-major-in-coaching-walk-on-chase-coleman-pursues-coaching-dreams-on-uva-s-sideline/article_7ffcde46-568e-11eb-8ca5-ff48492bd929.html (accessed Aug. 16, 2021).

9. Derrick Morgan, "My New Purpose," *Players' Tribune*, July 1, 2019, https://www.theplayerstribune.com/articles/derrick-morgan-titans-nfl-retirement (accessed Aug. 16, 2021).

10. "Alex Morgan, USWNT Players Appeal Decision against Equal Pay," *Sports Illustrated*, April 14, 2021, https://www.si.com/soccer/2021/04/14/uswnt-players-appeal-decision-against-equal-pay (accessed Aug. 16, 2021).

11. Nick Piastowski, "Bryson DeChambeau Gained Weight and Distance, and He LOST This," *Golf*, June 13, 2020, https://golf.com/news/bryson-dechambeau-gained-weight-distance-lost-this/ (accessed Aug. 16, 2021),

12. Joe Boozell, "History of 1 Seed vs. 16 Seed in March Madness," *NCAA*, January 28, 2019, https://www.ncaa.com/news/basketball-men/article/2019-01-28/history-1-seed-vs-16-seed-march-madness (accessed Aug. 16, 2021).

13. Anna Katherine Clemmons, "Net Positive," *UVA Magazine*, Summer 2019, https://uvamagazine.org/articles/net_positive (accessed Aug. 16, 2021).

14. Kevin Lane Keller, "Conceptualizing, Measuring and Managing Customer-Based Brand Equity," *Journal of Marketing* 57, no. 1 (January 1993): 1–22.

15. Kevin Van Valkenburg, "Deep in the Rough," *ESPN*, March 28, 2018, http://www.espn.com/espnw/feature/22858141/how-golfing-prodigy-lydia-ko-lost-way (accessed Aug. 16, 2021).

16. Parsons Xtreme Golf (@pxg), "'Believe in yourself, believe in your process and everything else will fall in place.' - Lydia Ko," *Twitter*, September 10, 2020, 3:23 p.m., https://twitter.com/pxg/status/1304138329630400512 (accessed Apr. 2, 2021).

17. "Lydia Ko's World Ranking Revival Continues," *Stuff*, September 15, 2020, https://www.stuff.co.nz/sport/golf/122771069/lydia-kos-world-ranking-revival-continues (accessed Aug. 16, 2021).

18. Simon Plumb and Felicity Reid, "The Private Life of Lydia Ko," *Stuff*, March 3, 2013, https://www.stuff.co.nz/ipad-editors-picks/8370287/The-private-life-of-Lydia-Ko (accessed Aug. 16, 2021).

19. Danielle Rossingh, "Novak Djokovic and the Adria Tour: The Exhibition Event That Shocked Tennis," *CNN*, June 27, 2020, https://www.cnn.com/2020/06/27/tennis/novak-djokovic-adria-tour-backlash-spt-intl/index.html (accessed Aug. 16, 2021).

20. Simon Cambers, "Novak Djokovic's New Union for Tennis Players Gets Low-Key Response," *Guardian*, June 26, 2021, https://www.theguardian.com/sport/2021/jun/26/novak-djokovics-new-players-body-gets-low-key-response (accessed Aug.16, 2021).

21. Amy O'Connor, "Martina Navratilova: 'If I Had Twitter 30 Years Ago, I Would Have Been Raising Holy Hell'," *Irish Times*, October 31, 2020, https://www.irishtimes.com/life-and-style/people/martina-navratilova-if-i-had-twitter-30-years-ago-i-would-have-been-raising-holy-hell-1.4392381 (accessed Apr. 2, 2021).

22. Andy Nesbitt, "Novak Djokovic Had a Classy Message for Roger Federer and Rafa Nadal after Wimbledon Win," *USA Today*, July 11, 2021, https://ftw.usatoday.com/lists/wimbledon-novak-djokovic-wins-classy-message-for-roger-federer-rafa-nadal (accessed Aug. 16, 2021).

23. Matthew S. Schwartz, "Novak Djokovic, the World's no. 1 Tennis Player, Fails to Medal at the Olympics," *NPR*, July 31, 2021, https://www.npr.org/sections/tokyo-olympics-live-updates/2021/07/31/1023184024/tokyo-olympics-novak-djokovic-loses-bronze-tennis (accessed Aug. 16, 2021).

24. Peter Bodo, "Novak Djokovic's Image Needs More Work Than His Tennis Game at US Open," *ESPN*, August 31, 2020, https://www.espn.com/tennis/story/_/id/29769338/novak-djokovic-image-needs-more-work-tennis-game-us-open (accessed Aug. 16, 2021).

25. Thuc Nhi Nguyen, "Nia Dennis Became UCLA's Latest Internet Sensation with Beyoncé-Inspired Floor Routine," *Los Angeles Times*, April 2, 2020, https://www.latimes.com/sports/ucla/story/2020-04-02/gymnast-nia-dennis-ucla-internet-sensation-floor-routine-beyonce (accessed Aug. 16, 2021).

26. "Tiger Woods Fast Facts," *CNN*, March 1, 2021, https://www.cnn.com/2013/05/30/us/tiger-woods-fast-facts/index.html (accessed Aug. 16, 2021).

27. Nick Piastowski, "How Tiger Woods Made $60 Million Without Hitting a Single Golf Shot," *Golf*, May 30, 2020, https://golf.com/news/tiger-woods-made-60-million-without-hitting-golf-shot/ (accessed Aug. 16, 2021).

28. Zac Johnson, "The Importance of Brand Loyalty and How to Improve It," *RingCentral* (blog), May 14, 2015, https://www.ringcentral.com/us/en/blog/the-importance-of-brand-loyalty-and-how-to-improve-it/ (accessed Aug. 16, 2021).

29. Garry A. Gabison, "The Gray Problem: Should Athletes Be Punished for Their Social Media Posts?," *DePaul Journal of Sports Law* 13, no. 1 (2017).

30. Alan Abitbol, "Razor Burned: Why Gillette's Campaign against Toxic Masculinity Missed the Mark," *The Conversation*, January 18, 2019, https://theconversation.com/razor-burned-why-gillettes-campaign-against-toxic-masculinity-missed-the-mark-109932 (accessed Aug. 16, 2021).

31. "New Data Reveals Consumer Skepticism When Brands Take a Stand," *Sprout Social*, November 5, 2019, https://investors.sproutsocial.com/news/news-details/2019/New-Data-Reveals-Consumer-Skepticism-When-Brands-Take-A-Stand/default.aspx (accessed Aug. 16, 2021).

32. Charles Kruger, "NBA Ratings Drop: New Poll Reveals Main Reason Why," *Game7*, September 8, 2020, https://itsgame7.com/nba-ratings-drop-new-poll-reveals-main-reason-why/ (accessed Aug. 16, 2021).

33. Hal Conick, "Consumers Want Brands to Take a Stand on Social Issues," American Marketing Association, *Medium*, October 2, 2018, https://medium.com/@AMA_Marketing/consumers-want-brands-to-take-a-stand-on-social-issues-46d8faea8c2 (accessed Aug. 16, 2021).

34. Chase Hughes, "Gill Makes Most of Rare Chance for Wizards," *NBC Sports*, April 24, 2021, https://www.nbcsports.com/washington/wizards/hard-worker-anthony-gill-makes-most-rare-chance-wizards (accessed Aug. 16, 2021).

35. Dana O'Neil, "Ever-Driven, Ty Jerome Is Shrewdly Fueling the Bounce-Back at Virginia," *Athletic*, January 17, 2019, https://theathletic.com/771318/2019/01/17/ever-driven-ty-jerome-is-shrewdly-fueling-the-bounce-back-at-virginia/ (accessed Aug. 16, 2021).

36. "Josh Allen Takes Responsibility for Tweets Sent as High Schooler," *ESPN*, April 26, 2018, https://www.espn.com/nfl/story/_/id/23325677/josh-allen-takes-responsibility-offensive-tweets-sent-high-schooler (accessed Aug. 16, 2021).

37. Kyle Newport, "Baker Mayfield Reportedly Agrees to 4-Year Rookie Contract with Browns," *Bleacher Report*, July 24, 2018, https://bleacherreport.com/articles/2773710-baker-mayfield-reportedly-agrees-to-4-year-rookie-contract-with-browns (accessed Aug. 16, 2021).

38. "Josh Allen," *Spotrac*, https://www.spotrac.com/nfl/buffalo-bills/josh-allen-25102/ (accessed Aug. 16, 2021).

39. All information taken from Fallon Sherrock's Twitter page, @Fsherrock, https://twitter.com/Fsherrock?ref (accessed Apr. 2, 2021).

40. All information on the different athlete bios came from the athletes' Twitter pages (all accessed Apr. 2, 2021).

41. Joe Leccesi, "Why Do Social Media 'Fails' by Young Athletes Keep Happening?," *USA Today*, High School Sports, May 1, 2018, https://usatodayhss.com/2018/why-do-social-media-fails-by-young-athletes-keep-happening (accessed Aug. 16, 2021).

42. Tanya Hall, "The New 80/20 Rule of Social Media Marketing," *Inc.*, November 16, 2018, https://www.inc.com/tanya-hall/the-new-80/20-rule-of-social-media.html (accessed Aug. 16, 2021).

43. Frank Urbina, "What Is the NBA's Minimum Salary?," *Hoops Hype*, https://hoopshype.com/2018/09/19/nba-minimum-salary/; Christina Gough, "NBA's Annual Salaries in 2019/20," Statista, October 7, 2021, https://www.statista.com/statistics/1120257/annual-salaries-nba/ (both accessed Aug. 16, 2021).

44. Michael McCann, "Inside the Rise of Michael Jordan's Unrivaled Marketability," *Sports Illustrated*, May 16, 2020, https://www.si.com/nba/2020/05/16/michael-jordan-mark

PRAISE FOR ATHLETE BRANDS

"This book coaches SAs to engage more effectively with Opendorse, agents, and others so that athletes can maximize NIL value well beyond their playing career by giving readers a process to identify, design, and activate their brands."

—*Blake Lawrence,* CEO of Opendorse, the leading NIL company

"NIL is the most disruptive and significant initiative to be introduced to the sports market in the last 40 years. Kim Whitler is one of the smartest and savviest brand marketers that I have met in my career and this book, based on her extensive experience and expertise, is a must for SAs looking to create, build, or enhance their brand. This book will help students to be thoughtful on what a brand is, what they want their athlete brand to be, and how they can activate their brand to achieve their short- and long-term goals."

—*Randy Eccker,* CEO of the Eccker Sports Group, former CEO and Chair of Circle Media and XOS Digital, named "one of the leading digital media and technology figures in the sports industry"

"The rights of SAs to monetize and profit from their name, image, and likeness has ushered in an era of tremendous opportunity for them. The lessons in this book offer essential learning not just for SAs, but for those who care most about their development: athletic directors, coaches, and parents. This book offers an easy-to-follow process that encourages SAs to think about their values and goals first, then the athlete brands they want to create to advance those goals, then ways to monetize their desired brands. In other words, it correctly puts the horse before the cart."

—*Ted White,* Founder/CEO of Fair Ball Foundation and Former Deputy Athletic Director, University of Virginia

---

"As a professional track coach and former college track and field coach, I've witnessed first-hand how student-athletes who build a strong reputation around hard work and dedication earn the respect of coaches and attention of sponsors. That can make all the difference when striving for a goal as lofty as the Olympics or even just transitioning from college to professional life. In the new NIL landscape, this book is an essential piece of the puzzle to help SAs balance their commitments to their education and the team while using their platform to pursue their dreams."

—*Adam Smith,* Assistant Coach, Reebok Boston Track Club; former assistant track and field coach at Syracuse University and University of North Carolina-Chapel Hill